CREATING GAIA CULTURE

VISION AND WORKBOOK

Marko Pogačnik
UNESCO Artist for Peace

CLAIRVIEW

Clairview Books Ltd.,
Russet, Sandy Lane,
West Hoathly,
W. Sussex RH19 4QQ

www.clairviewbooks.com

Published by Clairview Books 2021

Edited by Brain Newton

A CIP catalogue record for this book is available from the British Library

ISBN 978 1 912992 32 4

Cover by Morgan Creative featuring image © Marko Pogačnik
Typeset by Symbiosys Technologies, Visakhapatnam, India
Printed and bound by 4Edge Ltd, Essex

MARKO POGAČNIK was born in 1944 in Kranj, and lives in Šempas, Slovenia. He worked in Conceptual Art and Land Art as a member of the OHO group during the years 1965-71. He has had exhibitions in Aktionsraum, Munich, the Museum of Modern Art, New York, and Venice Biennale. After 1979 he worked in the field of art combined with integral ecology (geomancy). He has developed a method of Earth healing called 'lithopuncture', which utilizes stones complemented with carved 'cosmograms'. His works stand in many countries around the world, including in Europe, South & North America, Africa and Asia. After 1998 he developed Gaia Touch body exercises to tune to the essence of the Earth and its transforming process. His books in English include: *Nature Spirits & Elemental Beings, Touching the Breath of Gaia, Turned Upside Down, Gaia's Quantum Leap, Sacred Geography, The Universe of the Human Body* and most recently *Christ Power and Earth Wisdom* and *Dancing with the Earth Changes*. In 2016 he was appointed by the UNESCO Secretary General as Artist for Peace. Marko's website is www.markopogacnik.com

CONTENTS

ACKNOWLEDGEMENTS

The present book includes aspects of group working that should not be overlooked. Its editing was done by Brian Newton, one of the artists from our Geopuncture Installations team. The Gaia and Michael messages were received by Andrea Rosslan-Brandt in the German language and translated into English by Rachel Ries. The image on the front cover is my drawing of Gaia as Goddess, carved in stone by my wife Marika and photographed by Bojan Brecelj. Thank you dear friends!

Marko

PART 1: INTRODUCTION

Why this book?

Co-working during the last few decades intensely with the Earth and her beings, I dare to say that we are now at the threshold of a new phase of Earth's planetary evolution. Gaia and her elemental beings create breathtaking new conditions for life upon the planet, in tune with the future-promising evolutionary path of the universe. This is wonderful to know, even in the midst of rather distressing ecological situations that almost daily become worse. Yet the question arises: Do there exist human visions, ideas, and actions that would create a human culture, corresponding to the mentioned planetary transformation, that would also satisfy humanity's desire for a culture of peace and mutual understanding among people and nations?

In the past millennia, human beings—in general—have inwardly matured to a point that can be considered their adult stage of evolution. Unfortunately, we have taken a destructive path in the development of weapons, technology, and dangerous political and economic systems with the potential to destroy life upon Earth and the future of human culture. Instead we should be taking at this point full responsibility for our ideas, emotions, and creations—the proper sign of adulthood.

Together with the Earth and her beings, we find ourselves in the midst of a cosmic change that presents two conflicting realities. On the one hand, the present, material, three-dimensional world of nature and culture is deteriorating and disappearing. On the other hand, Gaia and her elemental helpers are creating new conditions for life. These new life-conditions cannot yet be seen or enjoyed as living reality, but by opening our perceptions to different levels of multidimensional reality we can experience them.

We should not stay behind! Even if the majority of humankind is still entangled in the disappearing world structures, we should not submit ourselves to lethargy. Instead, let us gather our experiences from the past and visions of the future and create an open matrix of a culture tuned to the recent development within the Earth and her cosmos.

This short introduction uncovers several reasons why the present book has a need to exist among billions of books written by the creative genius of the human family:

1. The book formulates the vision of a possible future human culture based upon co-creation with Gaia, her elemental worlds, and beings from parallel evolutions. It presents a utopian image of Gaia Culture, but also presents possibilities for the reader on how to collaborate with the process of its creation.

2. The book offers different exercises that can help the individual in developing needed sensibility, and the courage to practice a new level of perception that enables us to perceive beyond the rational borders that separate modern human beings from the wholeness of life.

3. The book offers the possibility to look into the primeval source of the future human culture by interpreting the ancient text of the Apocalypse in a completely new way. In the so-called 'Revelation of Saint John', the seed of—at that time—future Earth Changes, along with the vision of a new human culture are coded.

4. The book uses my experiences, visions, dream stories, communications with beings from the parallel worlds, peppered with 45 drawings and 40 meditative exercises, to help transcend the inherent mental structures, by triggering the quality of imagination within the reader. Imaginations can help the reader envision future human culture as an almost tactile reality, and actually help move this reality closer to manifestation.

Imagination is the basic tool of any creative process!

Gaia Culture vision

The idea to develop a Gaia-centred culture appeared unexpectedly during my flight from Venice to Lisbon in the year 2005. I travelled with my friend and collaborator Peter to Tamera, a human-ecological centre in the Evora region of Portugal, with an invitation to build a Geopuncture installation. We would work together with some members of the Tamera community, previously taught by Peter to carve stones and create 'Cosmograms'. A Geopuncture installation is a group of monolithic stones. Into each stone is carved a symbol with a message (a Cosmogram), that expresses the contained message not only through physical forms but also as a source of specific etheric energy movements coded in their concave forms.

The Geopuncture circle in Tamera is one of the first two installations of its kind, representing the start of a new collective art project. There are now 27 Geopuncture circles created in different land/cityscapes in Europe and in the American continent, comprising several hundred stones with carved cosmograms. Their purpose is to touch the body of the Earth at different points upon its surface with specific messages, thus developing a silent dialogue between the Earth—including its elemental worlds—and the human race.

It is not by chance that the idea for the Gaia Culture was born during a flight that ended with the creation of a Geopuncture circle themed 'Sociogram'—representing a complete presentation of the (ideal) human society. The Gaia Culture vision should, as a next step after the 'Sociogram', give an idea how human society could be transformed and become connected to the consciousness and to vital cycles of our home planet in a new way, comprising responsibility towards all aspects of life, visible and invisible.

Gaia Culture (alternatively Geaculture or Geoculture), according to the inspiration I received during a flight from Venice to Lisbon, is composed of three sequences:

1. The first of these sequences concerns the human being as an individual and the need to embody abilities that will enable us to

co-create, along with the living and conscious Earth, a culture of peace and togetherness. (Part 2 of the book)

2. The next sequence of the Gaia Culture plan is dedicated to relationships in human society—relationships built upon the above set of individual qualities. (Part 4)

3. The third sequence is dedicated to co-existence and cooperation of human individuals and our society with the beings of parallel evolutions that are part of the larger Earth that I call 'Earthly cosmos'. (Part 5)

Travelling through our Gaia Culture book will provide the opportunity to meet all three sequences and their different aspects and—most importantly—get a feeling for their essence and reality with the help of exercises positioned between the separate parts of the book.

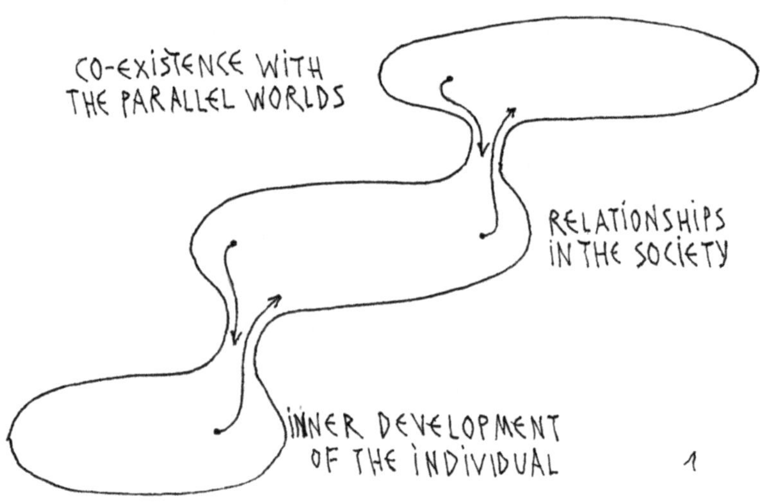

The three sequences of the future Gaia Culture

Why Gaia?

Gaia or Gea is the ancient Greek name for the Earth Goddess. We use it in modern times to make clear that the Earth is not just a clump of matter, nor is she a biosphere holder or just our home planet. The Earth is an autonomous being with a personal name: Gaia or Gea.

We are not interested in redefining the Greek system of Goddesses and Gods. If we give the Earth a Greek Goddess name, then it is to underline that she is a divine being with her own sphere of consciousness—the so-called 'noosphere'—that embraces all living creatures and beings, be they visible or invisible—the human family included.

Secondly, if we give the Earth a Goddess name, then it is to bring to awareness that Earth is actively and consciously taking part in the evolution of the whole cluster of worlds that she has created. She has created them with the intent to offer spaces to different sorts of beings and evolutions, spaces suitable for their development and for the unfoldment of their creative potentials.

The ignorance that modern human beings show towards the consciously active and loving nature of our home planet must come to an end if we want to continue to enjoy the hospitality of the Earth. The Gaia Culture project is a sincere attempt to offer possibilities to fellow human beings who have not yet experienced the love of the Mother of the earthly creation to change their attitude towards Gaia. It needs to be understood that the Gaia Culture project is not based upon a certain 'Gaia ideology' but offers—as in the case of this book—immediate experience of Gaia's sweet and inspiring presence with the help of various exercises.

Yet be aware that nobody can do the proposed exercises for you, dear reader. Everybody among us, interested in revivifying our relationship with Gaia and her elemental worlds, is responsible for performing the steps leading towards our goal for him or herself. In effect, this is the most precious gift on one's path of engagement to make our lives, and consequently, the lives of other beings, inwardly rich, peaceful, and happy.

Geomancy update

If we want to develop a more loving and cooperative relationship with Gaia, then it is not sufficient to just change our attitude towards her. We must also abandon the current narrow understanding of her planetary body that reduces her to material and biological aspects. It is a product of the rational approach to the Earth, fuelled by modern natural sciences, which persist in seeing the Earth as an object of scientific research. Such a superficial science-based approach intentionally avoids a heart-to-heart relationship with the Earth, maintaining a strict emotionless distance from Gaia, not recognizing her as a living being with her own history, presence, and purpose for existing.

Hope in changing our attitudes toward Gaia can be found in the rise of ecological awareness within the past century. The realization that the natural-science approach to the study of the Earth as an inanimate object has allowed it to be ruthlessly exploited, coupled with the disaster of so-called 'climate change', has led to rediscovery and up-to-date developments in the ancient science of geomancy.

Geomancy can be considered as old as human culture. It represents the knowledge of how human communities can position themselves in the diverse landscapes of the Earth, to become a part of their vital, elemental and spiritual dimensions. Geomantic knowledge has helped humankind harmoniously settle within the flow of Earth's vital powers without disturbing 'power places'. These places are necessary for sustaining life upon the Earth at its best conditions and permeating the planetary atmosphere with Gaia's primordial consciousness. The knowledge to identify the sacred places in the landscape was available to many different cultures. The places were honoured and strengthened through ritual and temple construction.

Geomancy still existed in the Middle Ages as a traditional science, along with alchemy, astrology, arithmetic etc. It disappeared with the rise of rational sciences. To be honest, it was *suppressed* during the time of the so-called 'witch hunts', between the fifteenth and eighteenth century. It reappeared, transformed as 'geology', examining

Gaia/Gea through a logical eye, closing off all but the visible world, suppressing any consideration of the sacred dimensions of the planet.

Since there were no written documents on the practice of medieval geomancy—touching upon the Earth in a spiritual manner was considered blasphemy by the Christian churches—we have had to raise modern geomancy from the ground up. Dowsing methods survived, and were used, as well as different methods of holistic perception of aspects of the Earth body hidden to the rational eye.

Basic to the understanding of up-to-date geomancy, is knowledge of the multidimensionality of Earth. The manifested worlds of plants, animals, minerals, and human beings are complemented by the 'causal' or 'archetypal' dimensions. It is in these dimensions that each manifested world phenomenon finds the matrix that forms and supports its life and purpose within the greater whole. The causal extensions of the Earth are partly focused in the core of the planet and partly rooted in the cosmic dimension of Gaia.

Considering the planetary level first, geomancy identifies the vital organism of the landscape with its network of vital-energy lines and centres. Of equal importance is the world of elemental beings, operating as fractals of Gaia's elemental consciousness, mediating between the causal and manifested halves of reality. Basic to the life of the Earth is the sub-elemental world, called by shamanic knowledge the 'underworld'. Dragons, the primeval creative powers of Gaia, work from this deep dimension of existence to sustain and nourish the vital conditions for the Earth, so that its cluster of worlds and beings can exist.

Related to the cosmic dimensions of Gaia, 'parallel worlds' should be mentioned. They can be considered as synchronic worlds existing parallel to each other. They enable development of different communities of beings that have chosen the Earth as the place of their learning and evolution. Among others, the ancestors and descendants from the human race find their autonomous space in Gaia's cluster of parallel worlds. The cosmic Gaia is also the origin of the so-called 'landscape temples' that represent the sacred dimension of the Earth and its different landscapes and biotopes.

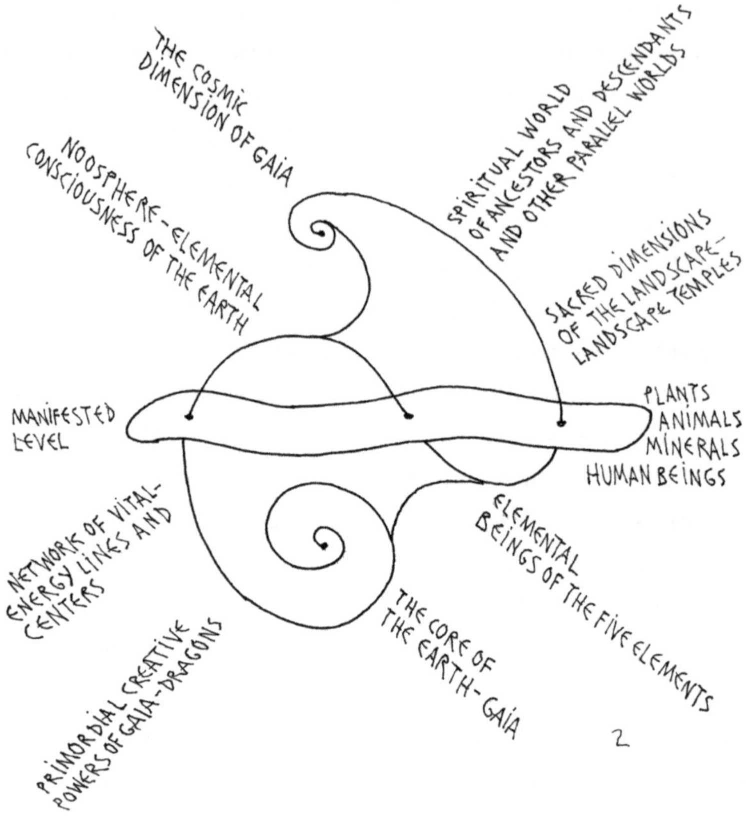

Relationship between the manifested Earth and the causal dimensions of Gaia

Holistic perception

The work of the essential deepening of human perception cannot be avoided if we want to develop a heart-to-heart relationship with Gaia and her elemental worlds. The five senses that humans usually use as their only window into their environment are not sufficient to perceive the reality of life in its entirety. Eyes, ears, skin, and other organs of perception were developed throughout millions of years so that we could have orientation in the world of matter and to be able to admire its beauties. Many thousands of animal species, be they birds, mammals, dinosaurs, fish etc., contributed their part in developing the so-called 'five senses' that we inherit when we are incarnated into the human body.

Unfortunately our modern culture has lost touch with the other types of perception known by the animal world. I speak of their sensitivity and instincts, used to orientate themselves within the subtle emotional and vital-energy fields in the landscape. I believe that they use these perceptions to remain in contact with other individuals of their species, with their group soul, and especially with Gaia and her elemental world.

If indeed the human race inherited our perfect organic senses from the animal kingdom, then we must also have inherited their subtle capacities to perceive the invisible features of the causal worlds. In effect we *have* inherited them! But in the last two millennia they have been heavily overlaid with the mental patterns produced by the human mind. Instead of opening itself to the subtle extensions of reality, the rational mind translates reality into its own logical language that is not transparent to reality existing beyond the boundaries set by physical world perception.

It is easily understood how our culture lost its loving and cooperative relationship with Gaia and her elemental worlds. The moment a subtle impulse reaches us—the touch of Gaia's presence for example— the rational mind recognizes it as impossible to be translated into the logical language and instantly closes the door to our awareness. One does not recognize that the Mother of life has touched one's heart. As a consequence, the vast majority of mankind believes that our space of reality is composed *only* of the physical and visible features.

This is clear; to regain the needed sensitivity to perceive the subtle dimensions of life, we have to abandon the control of the rational mind over our perceptions, thus clearing the way towards the freedom of perceiving the world in its wholeness. Each individual needs to set clear boundaries clarifying the domains of logical and psychic perceptions. Logical perception is needed to function within the manifested world. Psychic perception must be free to receive subtle impulses and for dialogue with Gaia and her subtle worlds. The tools needed for this kind of perception exist within each human being. We have at our disposal the sensitivity of our body and its aura, intuition for connecting to the field of the universal consciousness, and the human capacity of telepathic communication.

To help in the process of restoring your sensitivity, dear reader, I have created a number of exercises that appear in this book, together with short messages from Gaia received by Andrea, my collaborator from Germany. Exercises are accompanied by my drawings in the form of comics to make it easier to understand and memorize them. Another way, to redevelop one's awareness of subtle worlds, is by Gaia Touch body exercises. These presented tools are why our book functions as a workbook, not only to work on individual spiritual development, but simultaneously, on changing the world into a more satisfying place to live and to create in peace.

Earth's transformation story

The combination of renewed geomantic knowledge and widened perception has shown me that the Earth is presently moving through an intensive phase of inner change. I am not speaking of the so-called 'climate changes', but of the more profound Gaia transformation process of which changes in the planetary climate patterns are just one of its consequences.

The insight that Gaia was preparing a set of dramatic changes reached me through an extremely clear dream while in Geneva on 1 February, 1980. I was visiting my late friend Austin Arnold who was in service as British diplomat for the United Nations. The dream had four sequences.

In the first sequence I was told that a change is coming that was so complex that it will affect all aspects of life upon the Earth:

Sequence 1
I am walking with my friend along the shore of a lake watching ducks and swans as they bob among the waves. Suddenly I see the sky growing dark and heavy. Lightning strikes the lake with the forewarning of a mighty storm.

Sequence 2

I am led below the Earth's surface into a cave, illuminated from above by a flood of golden light. In the next moment, I am horror struck by the sight of a boy lying unconscious on the ground. The ice-cold water is flowing over his body's left side so that he is likely to freeze. I lift him up, press him to my heart and cry out: 'Where are his parents—he must get help!'

The second sequence showed me that the change happening inside the Earth would cause a dangerous lack of life energy at our level of existence. Some yet unknown cosmic event or process would cause the lifting of the flow of life to another frequency level. If human beings would not recognize the change, then we would not be able to adjust to the new conditions, thus losing connection to the network of vital energy—a precondition of our existence as embodied beings. The human race consequently would be in danger of becoming extinct, even as the planet was imbued with fresh, high-quality life force.

The message here was clear: to avoid the danger accompanying the incoming Earth changes, we need to recover the sensitivity to connect with Gaia's consciousness. This connection would activate the antennas necessary to tune to the new level of existence, allowing us to walk without hesitation along this unfamiliar path.

This second sequence of the dream inspired me to start working in the field of geomancy, rediscovering the forgotten knowledge of the multidimensional nature of our home planet. But soon I realized that the connection to the inner life of the Earth is not just lost, but heavily traumatized and blocked. Millennia of exploiting the Earth as an object of human rule and greed have caused deep wounds that would not allow us to reconnect with Gaia and to tune to her transformation process. This is why geomantic work with landscapes and places had to be complemented with what we rather improperly call 'Earth healing'. The intention is not to heal the Earth but to transform traumas and to remove blockades that blind human aggression has left upon the Earth body.

Sequence 3

My friend and I are in a dark hiding place, watching what is happening in an adjoining brightly lit corridor. We see a group of women walking there, making a specific gesture in front of their breasts. We cannot clearly see the gesture because they are moving small devotional objects in an intricate pattern with their gestures.

The third sequence of the Geneva dream concerns the basic change needed inside the human psyche to ready us for the approaching Earth transformation process. In the third sequence, criticism was revealed for the so-called 'New Age' spiritual movements. Their purpose was the development of spiritual practices, to heighten the consciousness level and inspire loving attitude towards fellow human beings. What they lacked was the quality of grounding. The immediate connection to Gaia was missing; also missing were acknowledgement of one's own elemental identity and the place of humankind in the matrix of life upon the Earth.

Sequence 4

While they are leaving the corridor, a young woman from their group turns around and runs to the entrance to our hiding place. Without noticing our presence, she lifts her tunic high over her shoulders and stands naked in front of us in all her beauty. Then with one clear movement she makes the gesture that we could not recognize when it was done in the group. She slides her index finger upward from her abdomen to her midsection between the breasts. Then lets her tunic fall back again and runs after the group.

For years I struggled for the correct interpretation of this last sequence. One aspect is obvious. We are encouraged to lift our relationship towards Gaia and her elemental worlds to a higher level of consciousness, marked by heart-to-heart relationships. The belly region stands for Gaia as the Mother of all-living—nourishing us, clothing us, and inspiring us to grow and expand our talents. The heart-connected relationship that she demonstrated upon her body is a cooperative one. Humankind should open their heart and share with Gaia and her elemental world the responsibility for the successful 'quantum leap' of our common world to the new evolutionary level.

The next push in the process of the Earth changes happened unexpectedly 28 years later—again announced through a dream—this time sleeping at home—on 4 November, 1997.

I run hither and thither among a crowd of people who, deep in their concerns, proceed in every possible direction, to cross a spacious city square. I cry out continually with all my strength, repeating a single sentence to which no one listens. No one even notices me. The sentence: 'We still believe that reality remains as it always was, but it's no longer true—what you see is only a memory of it!' I scream the words louder and louder till the sound of my voice wakes me up.

Shocked by the urgency transmitted by the dream I jumped out of the bed and ran outside to check the Earth's radiation. Here the next surprise awaits me. The radiation of the Earth, familiar to me from my geomantic work, has turned upside down! Instead of rising as high as my shoulder level it had flipped 180 degrees, reaching down into the Earth body.

Connecting my findings on the ground with the images of my dream, my conclusion is that the Earth now exists in two bodies that do not fit into each other. People in general still relate to the 'old' body, that for Gaia and her elemental worlds no longer exists. It persists as an appearance only in the memory of human beings supported by their elemental and spiritual helpers. The second Earth body, the 'new' one, exists at a deeper dimension of cosmic reality, different in its constitution. Humankind, trapped inside the mental structures of the rational mind, cannot perceive it, and thus continues to hold on to the old Earth that has no future.

I felt ethically responsible to carry the message of the birth of this new Earth among people—even though the dream warned me that it might find zero understanding among my fellow human beings. In the next 22 years, while observing the rather quick changes within the Earth body and Gaia consciousness, I have written a number of books, held countless lectures and workshops worldwide to spread the Earth-changing story update. I found many interested individuals but public response is still missing.

The scientific threat to life on Earth of 'climate change' directs the public and political awareness (and the corresponding flow of finances) in the wrong direction. All efforts go towards preserving the old Earth that Gaia and her creative powers no longer sustain. It seems that the so-called 'green policy' is driven by fear of changes approaching from realms of life that are seen as non-existent by the rational mind.

The second source of fear is certainly the unconscious-knowing that the Earth changes demand individuals to undergo a fundamental transmutation process, changing our mental patterns, psychic attitudes, social relationships... It seems easier to stay as we are despite multiplying natural catastrophes and pandemics we experience on a daily basis. And yet the solution is simple: listen to the sound of the cosmic process that Gaia and all her creation follows.

Embryo of the new planetary space

You may be interested in the next surprise upon the path of the Earth's dance of transformation. It happened 22 years later in the horrible year 2020. The year started with the Covid-19 pandemics that occupied humankind during the whole year and beyond. The pressure of the atmosphere felt like the pressure of a world war. Twice we went through a more or less severe 'lockdown', curfew during the night, and threat of death or being vaccinated with some unknown nano-materials...

During the same year something fantastic happened. Gaia, together with her spiritual and elemental helpers, has succeeded in manifesting the first models of the new reality on certain places of the planet. During the short time of August and September, when we were permitted to travel, I visited three such places, where I lead geomantic and Earth healing workshops. One of them I found in Italy, one in Germany, and the third in Switzerland.

What do I mean by a model of the new reality? A model, we think of as a three-dimensional object, to prepare for the next creative phase where the model gets translated into immediate reality—a building, for example, can be built following a preconceived model. In our case, it means that Gaia has gotten far enough in her process to manifest a multidimensional space as the basic model for the new Earth body.

It is not the last step in the Earth changing process, but it is an important one. From this moment on, the Earth exists as two separate and yet interconnected realities and we, embodied beings, take part in two spheres of reality at the same time. On one side we live in the materialized world that we know well, and on the other we move through a subtle, still invisible space that inherits the capacity to transport life and all its beings towards the future. Now we must jump constantly from one to the other. We need to accomplish our duties in the 'old' world, take children to school and function as citizens. Simultaneously—if we want to continue existing—we need to ground ourselves in the new space, perform our needed inner changes, tune to diverse worlds that constitute the new cluster of the Earth etc.—without losing our unique identity.

This is exactly the situation experienced when I visited Venice on 10 January, 2020. I observed crowds of tourists walking the narrow streets or in the luxury of being paddled in a gondola… perhaps visiting churches and marvelling at their artistic wealth. At the same time, I walked through Venice as a body of light, colour, and movement. After working almost 40 years in Venice, exploring its geomantic phenomena, I am very familiar with the invisible (causal) aspects of almost each place in the city. But this time I was not attracted by separate places and their secrets. This time I realized that I was moving inside a completely separate space from the 'official' Venice, but no less complete and beautiful. I had the feeling of walking inside an embryo that Gaia still holds in her womb, but looks ready to be born. Each of the sacred places of Venice has still a specific role to play in the subtle organism of the city, but at the same time, each represents one organ of the future planetary space.

I would love to take you to Venice and show you the embryo of the new planetary space being built. But even now, writing these lines on 14 December, 2020, Venice is still closed to visitors. Also I would need to first introduce you to the geomantic knowledge about this unique water city before presenting to you the seed of the new space as it manifests in Venice. This would be far too much information and experience for a single visit/workshop. (If you read German this seed is presented in my book, *Venedig als Samen des neuen Erdraums.*)

Instead I would like, dear reader, to take you directly to the workshop where Gaia and her elemental helpers work on building the new planetary space. In effect we are here interested in that department of Gaia's workshop where the seed of the new planetary culture is being designed and built. I call it 'Gaia Culture'.

EXERCISES 1

With Gaia messages and imaginations from Andrea Rosslan-Brandt

Now we are ready to start our workbook programme. Do not jump over this part of the book. If you would not like to work right now, then at least have a look at some of the Gaia messages received by Andrea during the preparation for this Gaia-Culture book. Beginning 12 November, 2020, Andrea received a daily message from Gaia. And I, Marko, created a corresponding imagination/exercise the following day. I later drew accompanying comics for each exercise, to facilitate your memorizing of the imaginations. So as not to overwhelm you with work, I have distributed the Gaia messages and my exercises/imaginations in several places throughout the book.

Andrea Rosslan-Brandt was born in 1968 and lives in Herne, Germany. We began to collaborate in the year 2013 when she invited me to the Hibernia Waldorf School in Herne where she works, to present one of my books. Since then, she has annually organized my workshops and book presentations in Ruhrgebiet, Germany.

Andrea writes with her right hand. But in 2019 she felt an energy in her left arm and an intuition to have trust to write with the left hand, something she had never done before. Following a meditation, she felt as if she had fallen into Gaia's embrace, and a pencil was pushed into her left hand, accompanied by the following words:

Write, write healing words. Put questions and write.

The words heal with their touch. Touch causes healing. Do it.

At the beginning of November, 2020, I invited Andrea to collaborate with the present book project, thus offering her left-hand writings to the public. Interestingly, the first short Gaia text of Andrea's seemed to contain a corresponding exercise. After receiving each morning text from Andrea, I sit down, close my eyes, and the imaginations needed to create a corresponding exercise begin to arrive.

I propose to the reader to choose an exercise and do it for a few days, perhaps writing down the experiences to ground your work properly. Be aware that it is not a selfish act to work on these exercises alone. You are working with Gaia. Based upon the living words of Gaia, the exercises contain the power to inspire the collective energy-field of humankind towards a deeper connection with Gaia and towards better understanding of the sources of life.

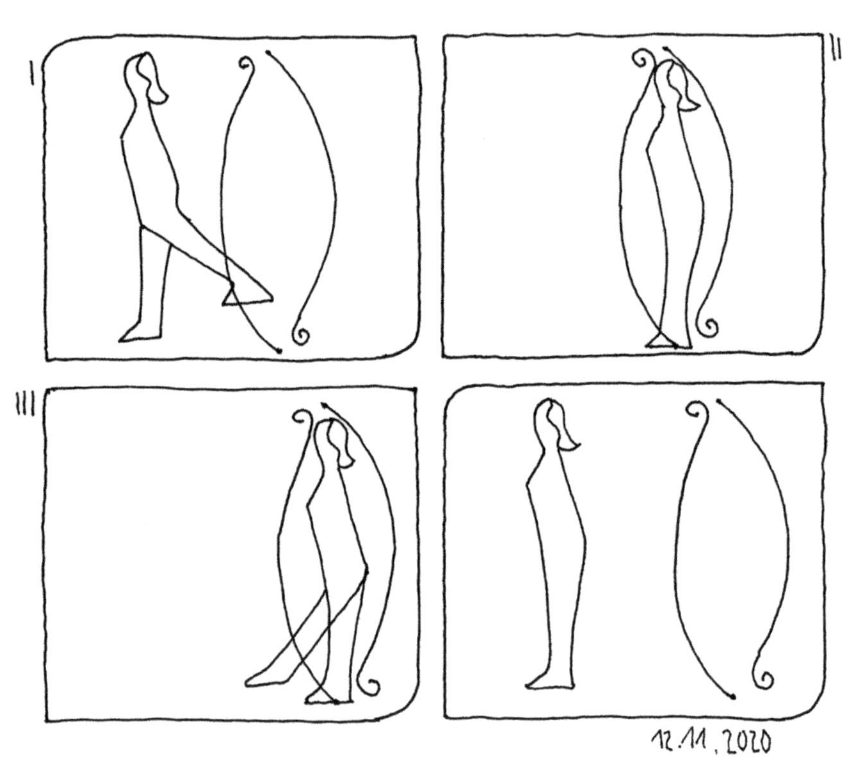
I
II
III
12.11.2020

12.11.2020

When you humans
approach your inner peace,
we—humanity and earth—experience
how close and connected we become.
And then,
then you awaken to our Oneness.
(Gaia)

- This exercise is done standing up.
- Imagine that the Mother of Life is standing behind your back.
- Try not to form a picture of her, but let the feeling arise in you of how it feels when the Mother of All Life is being addressed.
- Take a step backwards with your left foot so that you are standing within her presence for a while.
- Then, take a step forward with your right foot so that you are back in your body.
- Now look, feel, how the power and beauty of Gaia affects your body.
- Pay close attention to what the quality of your body space feels like, from the soles of your feet to above your skull.
- Repeat the exercise a few times to deepen your relationship with Gaia, the Mother of Life, and the relationship with your body.

14.11.2020

14.11.2020

The threshold of death—
not physical death.
The old selves go,
leaving the metamorphosing human being.
Newly turned to the spiritual realms,
many people have found ways
back into the 'All One'—the Source.
Human beings, recognize your true essence: your 'I am'
and seize your mission—
You are mediators between heaven and earth.
(Gaia)

- This exercise is done standing up.
- Lift your legs, one after the other, as if you were striding forward, but remain in place. Continue this marching movement.
- Death is walking towards you, from the front.
- It passes you, lightly brushing your right shoulder as it passes.
- Continue the marching movement.
- Death recedes further and further behind you.
- In doing so, it transmutes as much as possible of the impurities and injustices that you left behind.
- As you move forward you are surprised at how much clarity and joy death has left behind as it passed through your future.
- Sit down now and immerse yourself in this joyful vision of the future and the past.

15.11.2020

15.11.2020

Human being, only true inner self-affirmation
will allow you entirely to feel into our bond,
for a new time of unity
which is now dawning.
Without your intrinsic 'yes', our oneness remains only a vision—
  unattainable.
Show yourself to me, Gaia.
I love you.
Human, awaken into your existence.
(Gaia)

- Imagine a lake in your heart space.
- The heart space is dark rather than light.
- A drop falls from the centre of your cranial space onto the surface of the lake with the message 'Awaken!'.
- Then another drop, and another... until the lake opens up and the golden sphere of your true being rises from the depths and begins to shine.
- Your rays touch the forests in the distance, the birds in the sky, the mountains in the distance...
- ...to finally embrace Gaia as the Mother of all Being.

16.11.2020

16.11.2020

Human being, open your eyes, wake up.
Waking up, staying awake;
and after the awakening:
you are free to take the next step.
We are ready to guide you.
Christ in you.
(Gaia and Michael)

- Imagine you are standing in the middle of a simple rounded temple, which is closed off with a triangular roof gable.
- Look towards the floor of the temple and realize that you are standing on a mirror.
- In the mirror on the floor you see the triangle of the gable, which represents the divine expansion of the universe, aligned with the heart of the Earth.
- Become aware that the Divine exists, not only in the universe but also in the centre of the Earth.
- Bend down, take a fractal (holographic particle) of the divine heart of Gaia and let your hand bring it into the temple of your heart, to feel it and to offer Gaia's heart a second home in your heart.

18.11.2020

18.11.2020

Human being, welcome yourself into your
own life.
See this gift—a life, your life.
Preserve it, guard it, respect and cherish it.
Learn to rest within yourself, so that this peace that is more and more
living in you, will increasingly
enable you to allow our connection.
(Gaia)

- Go into the silence and seek to recall from your memory a forest where beautiful healthy trees grow.
- Invite one tree at a time to form a circle around you.
- Listen to the light rustle of their crowns.
- In doing so, you go deeper and deeper into your centre to experience inner peace.
- Take time to consolidate the silence within you.
- The trees around you support you in building a loving relationship with Gaia in this silence.

20.11.2020

20.11.2020

Human beings—here you are, standing in our connectedness
and you can feel your stability.
Through our bond you offer your open heart to me.
This is where we experience intimacy and the feeling of being at home
in our oneness.
(Gaia)

- Imagine standing in front of the door to your warm home.
- Outside, the pelting rain is driven by the howling wind. It is cold.
- The door opens and you step over the threshold with your right foot. (Make the gesture forward with your right foot.)
- But the left foot does not want to follow. Now you are standing between the outer world, which is sinking because of crises, and the warmth of Gaia and her elemental beings who know the future of life in the new world.
- Make up your mind!
- Take the step over the threshold and thus make the gesture that unites the left and the right foot.
- Take the time to experience what it feels like to stand in the warmth of Gaia's love.

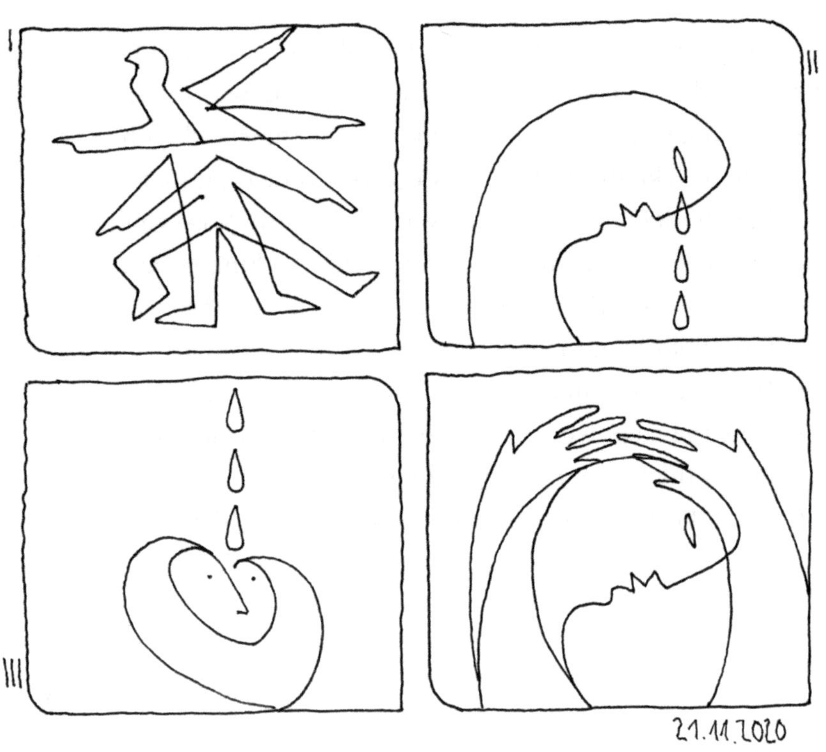

21.11.2020

21.11.2020

Human being—dare, permit yourself
to encounter yourself
in my embrace.
Let go, here with me.
Behind the veil of all your tears
I will reveal myself to you.
(Gaia)

- Modern humans have an excessive number of tasks. Everything around us demands our attention.
- When you perceive yourself straying from your spiritual mission, imagine that on the inside there is a second 'you' who is incessantly crying.
- Its tears seep so deeply into the Earth that they touch the heart of Gaia.
- In the warmth of Gaia's heart, they evaporate and their vapour rises back to you as her motherly love.
- Attend to this process in order to dissolve the armour of your alienation.

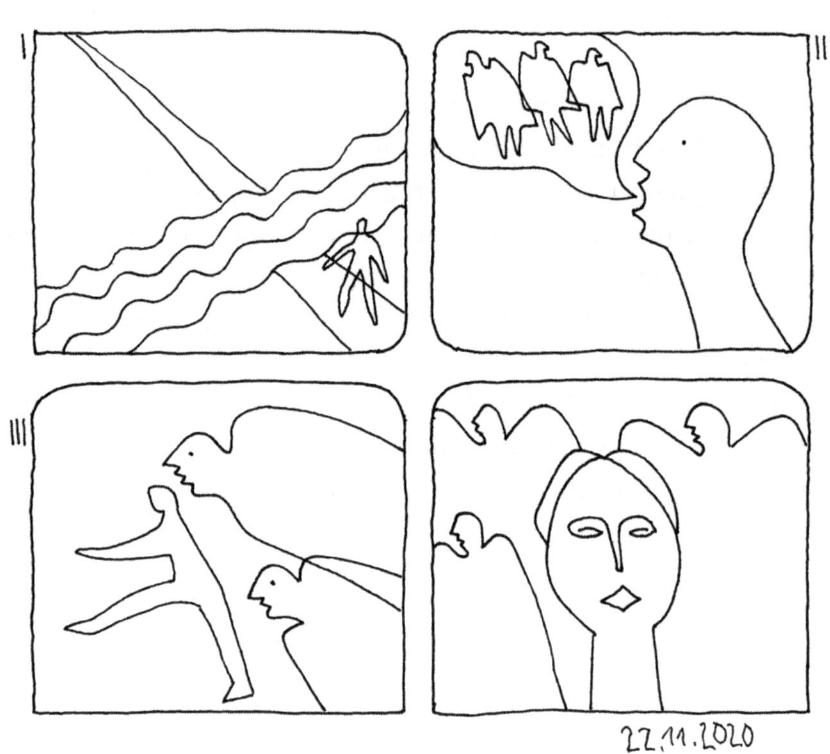

22.11.2020

22.11.2020

Human beings, allow yourselves to ask for help.
Hold the companions,
who departed from you in the physical world, in remembrance.
They are here.
They are ready and expecting you, in order to escort you further.
Just turn towards them and
you will receive their accompanying blessing
and their support for your earthly journey.
From their present spiritual realm they speak to you:
'Awaken'.
(Gaia)

- Imagine that you are standing on the bank of a wide, deep river.
- Your path in life could continue on the opposite shore, but how do you get there?
- Now summon some of the deceased people you know from your personal life or from collective memory.
- Feel them by your side and then cross the great water.
- Take time to feel how close they are and how helpful their support can be when you are faced with difficult moments in your life.
- Use this experience when such moments try to knock you down.

PART 2: GAIA CULTURE—INDIVIDUAL ASPECTS

The existing human civilization leaves behind its 'glorious expansion': destroyed landscapes of the Earth and much of its population entangled in warfare and starving. Even acknowledging that there are dedicated individuals and organizations that work to keep peace among nations while helping the poor, we are being taught a basic lesson: it is not possible to create a culture of peace and mutual understanding—even with the best intentions—unless each individual is truthful to her or his own essence, no matter how they choose to express themselves: words, action, or creativity. This is the reason why we start our discovery of the future human culture by giving attention to the human being as an individual.

It is not my intention to teach you. My hope is that together, we will trace one possible path, leading towards a future human being, free of past burdens and capable of co-creating the Earthly cosmos together with Gaia, her elemental helpers, and the spiritual worlds.

Do not look upon my efforts critically, as opposition to scientific knowledge or as a kind of esoteric ramble. Please understand them as imaginations, based upon the experiences of a crazy artist. They should not be believed-in, but rather looked upon as creative material to work with, while following a clear intention: we want to live in a culture that offers to each individual the best conditions for inner development and creative expression according to her or his needs—without harming other beings and dimensions of the Earthly cosmos.

A hymn to peace

The peace I am referring to is not primarily the maintaining of an attitude of silence within. Peace is a universal quality, a complex sound that permeates the whole universe—its star systems and beings.

It could be described as the constant roaring of the ocean coupled with the sweet sound of the celestial harmonies. To be at peace means to be in tune with this powerful yet harmonious sound, as one's constant inner reality.

To experience the bliss of this universal peace, one must first silence the constant chattering of mental patterns in one's head. We cannot avoid taking part in the affairs of the alienated world around us, thus losing the quality of the inner silence from moment to moment. But a persistence of silence within cannot be damaged by the outer rumours, if in the background we stay connected to the sound of the universal peace.

Please sit down now and try the following imagination:

- Keep the head in silence.
- Imagine the sound of the sea waves when they hit the rocky seashore vibrating in your belly region—the pelvic cavity.
- In your heart space vibrates the harmonious sound of classical music—like Vivaldi or Mozart.
- Let the sound of the belly region rise to the level of the heart while lowering the sound of the heart space down towards the pelvic cavity.
- Be the synthesis that comes into being when both vibrations meet and fuse in the plexus area.
- Listen to the sound of peace and then distribute it throughout your body, the head included.

The soul connection

At this point, I feel the need to introduce the idea of the individual human soul and the importance to be in touch with one's soul aspect. To again become a race of truthful and loving beings, we need to find ways of reconnecting to our soul aspect.

But I am reluctant to introduce the idea of the soul because it has a number of fixed meanings that prevent the free approach to one's own soul essence. To avoid all possible side paths that do not connect to the essence, I ask you to take part in the following imagination:

- Imagine holding in your hands a beautiful and healthy fruit—the apple might be the most suitable because of its archetypal connotations.
- Slip inside that apple and be that apple. Feel its purity, its pure light, not a dry light, but one permeated by the Water of Life.
- The soul is that dimension of the human being that holds upright the matrix or archetype of who we are individually, beyond the time and space barriers and beyond the mental concepts of who we are as eternal souls.
- While holding the archetypal apple in your hands, be aware that your soul is not only a being of light, but is also imbued with the Water Element of Gaia. This is the outcome of our age-long interaction with Gaia and her elemental worlds during our embodiment upon the planet.

To be truthful and loving in any situation means to perceive the given situation in the living and pulsating light-and-water of the soul—in effect to walk through the venues of life constantly perceiving reality in the mirror of the primeval purity and sensitivity of the soul. In this sense, our soul body can be equal to a child bursting with life and joy sitting in the lap of the divine Mother. But this child stays always a child, throughout our whole life, holding the purity of our divine origin within, plus the knowledge of who we are individually and the purpose of our existence in the universe.

Walking the path of change

Awaiting incarnation, the human being exists as a holographic unit of the spiritual world. We are part of the large community of human souls existing beyond the manifested space and time dimensions. We next find ourselves face to face with ourselves as embodied beings walking the path of incarnation together with minerals, animals and plants.

- Imagine yourself sitting with a beloved animal in your lap.
- Hold a piece of stone in one hand; the other embraces a pot with a growing plant.
- Imagine sitting like this in a cave under the Earth.
- How does it feel to be a member of the embodied Gaia family?

As souls, we incarnate again and again into the Earth's organic body to work on developing the world of matter. Like divers in the ocean depths searching for oysters with pearls, we come down into the manifested world searching for its secrets and its beauty. After a while the diver's breath is gone and he needs to ascend to get fresh air. Similar in our case—after several decades also our breath is gone and we need to leave the earthly plane to get some fresh air in the halls of eternity.

As you have accepted to dive into the chaos of the manifested world, you have also committed to accepting the constantly changing cyclic nature of that world. The seasons of the year change, the star constellations continuously shift, your psychic and spiritual body changes according to your inner development, and *Gaia's universe changes according to the cosmic cycles.* Aware or unaware, we are incarnated at this time in human development to cooperate with Gaia and her elemental world during the transition from the epoch of the 'Earth' Element into the epoch of the Element 'Air'.

During the epoch governed by the Element-Earth, Gaia and her elemental helpers have succeeded in translating life power into the dense form of matter. Together with plants, animals, and minerals we can, in recent times, enjoy the beauty of an incarnated planet and experience the challenge of manifesting our ideas and life patterns into material form.

Now, the cosmic cycle changes—find more about the background of this unique change in my book, *Dancing with the Earth Changes.* The position of the Earth-Element, as the ruling principle among the Four Elements, is being taken over by the Air-Element. The difference between the two Elements seems enormous. But considering that the Element-Air stands for the quality of consciousness, it will never 'rule' alone, but always in cooperation with the other three, including the Earth-Element, that will continue to hold responsibility for grounding.

The qualities that Air brings, make the creation of a balanced and peaceful Gaia Culture possible. These are the qualities of movement between different levels of existence, the borderless dance of creativity, the freedom to be who we are…

Honour to the Personal Elemental Being

The embodied human being would be a formless cloud, composed of countless cells, atoms, microorganisms etc., if there would be no cooperation between the individual soul and the Personal Elemental Being. According to my insight, the soul, before entering the path of incarnation, makes a 'contract' with a chosen elemental being to accompany her during the whole span of her embodied life.

There are different ways to explain elemental beings. They can be understood as holographic units or fractals of Gaia, operating in the field between the invisible (causal) and manifested (embodied) worlds. They are part of Gaia's all-embracing consciousness, giving them the knowledge to piece together the building blocks of Gaia's creations (atoms, cells, microorganisms, viruses etc.) and embodying her creations with their proper forms, dynamics, and vital conditions.

But it is important to understand that elemental beings do not work shaping anything from outside. While manifesting the creation of Gaia, giving it the proper form—be it physical or etheric—the elemental beings need to be embodied inside that being—a plant, a stone, an animal or a human being—forming it from inside out. In the case of a tree, for example, its elemental being moves within its watery streams reaching to the highest twig and to the deepest root. Similar in the case of a human being: the Personal Elemental Being is present in all the extensions of our multidimensional body. We share our body with a chosen elemental being who represents the wisdom of Gaia that takes care for all expressions of her creation.

- Please close your eyes for a moment and imagine that all your atoms, microorganisms, and cells are freely suspended in the air.

They float among the microorganisms, atoms, and cells of your environment.

- To recreate your body, the Personal Elemental Being is called in each successive moment to identify those atoms, cells and microorganisms that belong to you, fit them properly together and allowing their exchange with the environment—a fantastic achievement of his Gaia-connected consciousness.

It is an over-simplification to say that we, as human beings, are part of nature. This statement is superficial because it does not express how deeply we are involved in the creation of nature, accompanied in each moment by the elemental world. We take our makeup for granted. If we were unattended by the Personal Elemental Being for even a split second, we could dissolve into billions of pieces, lost among innumerable atoms, microorganisms, viruses and cells of our environment. I believe that our dependence on the elemental beings to secure the manifested world is the reason aboriginal cultures called Gaia the Mother of the Earthly creation.

To embody the primordial love

The quality of love can be experienced at different levels. It can be love pulsating between family members, love of the mother to her children, emotional love connecting a couple, love of one's homeland etc. But if we speak of love that is able to support the emergence and existence of Gaia Culture, then it should be thought of as primeval love. It is a quality of love as strong as a dragon and as soft as the morning breeze.

Primeval love is not easy to define with words of logic. (I wrote this sentence last night and was stumped on how to continue. It was late so I decided to sleep on it.) That night I had a dream that I thought might help me to express the difficult-to-express:

> *I enter a sanctuary with a triangular tympanum at the top. I notice that the ceramic pot with the plant, positioned at the highest point of the temple, is missing and I make the temple custodian aware.*

It is a plant with long beautiful green vines hanging down—a domestic variation of asparagus. I go home—just around the corner. Entering my room, I am surprised to find a ceramic piece of the asparagus pot lying on my floor. It is against logic that a ceramic piece of the smashed pot could land in my room from around the corner!

The asparagus, at the highest point of the (cosmic) temple, represents love, as the quality making the existence of the universe, its beings, and civilizations possible. One can imagine the network of primeval love, represented by the ceramic pot, holding the universe and its evolutions in perfect unity and co-creative diversity, both at the same time. The dream shows that human beings have a special gift, of which we are not entirely aware. We carry in our hearts a fractal of the primordial love (the shard of pot in the dream). I believe the purpose of having this gift is to raise us, step by step, to become loving and conscious co-creators of the future universe.

The hostility or even cruelty that people often show to each other—in wars for example—could be a consequence of our subconscious fear of embodying this immense divine gift—fear of a psychic situation we could not handle. It could also possibly be an influence of foreign powers that know the secret of the human heart. Since most people are unaware of this power, others might be able to influence its quality for their own selfish purposes. By turning around the holographic piece of the primeval love into something extremely negative, they can suck the sweetest 'juice' of the universe from the human heart.

How can we protect the fractal of divine love embodied within the (organic/etheric) space of our heart to be free of abuse? Each of us carries within our body a spark of the cosmic love. I believe that we, as human beings, need to inwardly expand our bodies to encompass the power of this spark within its own dimension.

I will speak now about the need to awaken the quality of the giant within us. I do not mean some foreign being of gigantic dimensions, but the quality of a giant that we inherit. I suppose that we inherit it from a race of beings that were human predecessors upon Earth from time immemorial—possibly Atlantis. They have introduced to the planet the role that we should play in the time ahead or even now. I speak of the task to maintain the connection between the immense expansion of the Galaxy and the 'tiny' Earthly cosmos. Here is an exercise to experience the giant within:

- While standing, bow down and imagine reaching with your fingers under your feet—not physically even if you could.
- Stay for a while like this. Then stand up imagining that your fingers stay positioned under your feet. This means that your arms are now much longer.
- To achieve the proper proportion between your arms and your body, you need to grow to the stature of a giant. Allow this growth to happen within you.
- Now your body as a giant corresponds to the immense cosmic power concentrated in your heart.
- (According to the rule of resonance, the exercise can be used also to perceive giants in the landscape or to connect with ancient trees.)

Once awakened within oneself, care must be taken to not misuse the power of the inner giant for selfish purposes!

Renew your sensibility

As stated in the Introduction, the five senses most humans depend on as their window into the environment are not sufficient to perceive the reality of life in its entirety. Eyes, ears, skin, and other organs of perception were developed throughout millions of years to orient us in the world of matter, while giving us the tools to admire its beauties.

The 'five senses' are a wonderful gift from Gaia and the animal kingdom. Problematically, during the past millennia of patriarchal rule and later dependence on scientific methods, a mental block was formed that says nothing exists that cannot be perceived through the five senses. As a result, rationality completely controls the perception process of most modern human beings, assuring that intuitive insights and subtle feelings have no influence on the human experience. The moment the rational mind is touched by a subtle vibration, the perceiver's mind identifies it as a threat to its one-sided logical world and swiftly declares it as non-existent. Hence, the human race feels assured that nothing exists beyond the horizon of intellectual discourse.

My advice to overcome the described situation is to teach the rational mind to step aside for a moment and allow intuition to read the message first. It takes no more than a split second for complex information to be received in its entirety. Only after receiving the message, the mind should be allowed to enter the process and work on decoding the perceived message, translating it into a logical statement.

There is no reason to suppress the logical mind. Rather it should be moved from the first to the last place in the perception process. We must persist in our human right to perceive reality in its multidimensional wholeness. Without holistic perception, insights into the actual state of the Earth's transformation process and the helping hands of the parallel worlds will seem not to exist.

For holistic perceptions to become as reliable as our five senses, preconditions must be set. The concept of subject-objective distance between the observer and the observed must be abandoned. Multidimensional perception functions only if the observer lovingly becomes one with the observed. Perceiving a tree for example; you should identify with the tree—be one with it—while allowing the tree to exist within you. You will be blessed by experiencing the inner dimensions of the tree. The tree will feel blessed by the insight into the human universe. Also the tree should be enriched in the perception process, not just the human observer.

One should not aim for objective results when practising holistic perception. The multidimensional reality is as much objective as it is subjective. Do not fear interacting in the process of perception. On the contrary, holistic perceptions can come into being only if you creatively cooperate with the process through which perception of reality comes into being. The received information is usually pure vibration and will not speak to you or anyone else if you do not allow your intuition and imagination to give it proper form and expression.

By being subjectively involved in the creation of the manifested world, the reality of life again becomes filled with love and light. We human beings become inspired to take responsibility for our co-creation with Gaia. Even more, holistic perception guarantees the reality of life will continue to exist in the renewed Earth body.

To become more feminine

Bringing forth Gaia Culture will require a step-by-step process of the masculine face of the human being retreating, while bringing our feminine aspect more forward. This is possible since each human being is of masculine and feminine gender, even if we outwardly look female or male. If we appear as a man, then it is because our masculine aspect is (only!) three to ten per cent stronger then the feminine—and vice versa.

Walk with me through the following exercise to help balance the relationship between your two aspects:

- If you are a woman, then you look forward through your feminine face while your masculine face looks backward—vice versa if you are a man.
- If you are a woman, then your body faces the light of the manifested world while your masculine body exists in the night of the causal (archetypal) world—vice versa if you are a man.
- Take some time to feel this ideally balanced relationship between your masculine and feminine aspects.
- Now turn around in your imagination and embrace your invisible partner. (Perhaps you have ignored her/him too long.)

The tragedy of the past and present patriarchal (men dominated) era is that its governing matrix gives excessive power to the masculine aspect, even if the given person is of feminine gender. As a result, in the modern world we are faced with excessively rich persons, excessively aggressive rulers, and hardened managers—not always of the masculine kind.

In entering Gaia Culture, we will work together with Gaia and her elemental consciousness to create a new matrix of life that is permeated with feminine principles and qualities, making a new kind of balance with the masculine possible. It is not about repairing the old system. We need to acknowledge the negative experiences of the past patriarchal era, but also realize that the masculine side has important qualities that we cannot discard. But it is time for the masculine-feminine (yang-yin) relationship to be flipped. Feminine qualities must be moved to the forefront as our guiding principles on the path to the future.

Do we now enter an era of feminine *rule*? No, because it is the nature of the feminine principle to seek wholeness, and with it, demand that the masculine qualities are always included—but this time, not as rulers but co-creators.

What does it mean, practically, that we are about to move into a feminine evolutionary era? It means, for example, that decisions, planning, and execution are not made along a linear path. The feminine approach demands at least a split second invested in attuning the consequences to the universal family of any plan. *Is this plan in tune with the purpose of my soul and the intuition of my heart?*

Feminine kind of action starts with a moment of peace. The process goes inward first. This process is a thousand times more effective then masculine aggressiveness, because it draws on the power and intelligence of parallel worlds. They need a point of entry to help with the process of co-creation. This is offered to them with a moment of attunement. Feminine planning tunes to the cosmic momentum, allowing a more holistic process, with much less effort.

It is not possible to play harmonious music with an instrument that is out of tune. It is tricky to move through the world without being grounded and attuned. Here is an exercise to help you tune:

- Stand up and slowly lift your hands as high as you can.
- Imagine while lifting your hands up, to simultaneously let them fall down towards the core of the Earth. (You stand head up and head down!)

- For a moment you stand with hands pointing both towards Heaven and towards Earth.
- Then bring all 'four' hands to the level of your heart, breathing-in the quality of attunement.

Protect the body

Please do not allow your human body, developed through the efforts of countless animal species, to be taken away from you! I sense a hidden plan—with the help of sophisticated machinery and electronic intelligence, in cooperation with detailed scientific research of your body's physiological functions, reaching from muscles to cell organization—to restitute our animal body with a robot body. It is true that the body we inherited from animals is not perfectly constructed or eternally enduring. But do we need such perfection if our purpose on Earth is to be taught lessons of embodiment and the knowledge of how to create in the conditions of the divine dimension of matter? We learn much through making mistakes that are mirrored in consecutive body issues and illnesses.

The body that we inherit from the animal kingdom is not just a physical body. It is not just about the perfection of its bodily organs. Look at the perfect possibility to perform in modern ballet or observe female and male professional athletes! The body we inherit is premier artwork of Gaia and her elemental hands. It was perfected first upon highly evolved animals, walking the solid ground of the five continents. Only afterwards were we human beings invited to start our endless cycles of incarnation. Paleontology gives proof that, during the past millions of years, the ape body was indeed fantastically developed through our conscious use and with help from the spiritual world of ancestors and descendants.

Instead of discarding the gift of Gaia and the animal sphere, we should feel free to work on the existing body, developing it to a next phase of its sensibility and viability. Neurologists say, for example, that today we use only a few per cent of our brain capacity. This is one sign of the potential our human body has yet to tap. Esoteric anatomy knows several subtle bodies that could be better integrated into the material-body level. The existing body could be developed so that humans could enter the inter-dimensional portals and navigate with our physical body—not just in our imagination—through subtle dimensions of the parallel worlds, to learn more about the secrets of life.

Parallel identities

Later we will dedicate Part 5 of our book to the theme of the parallel worlds of Gaia. In this section, the Earth is presented as a cluster of parallel worlds that ideally complement each other; unfortunately not acknowledged by present human culture, which has closed itself into one logically-comprehensive world sphere, considered the only sphere in existence.

Something similar can be said relating to our individual human identity. We have identity cards, passports, and other documents that fix our identity in the space and time between our birth and death. Officially, this is our only valued identity. Of course the aspect of the human being, related to our daily life and practice, is the ground aspect of our identity. I compare this with the touchable Earth globe and its role in the cluster of Gaia's parallel or synchronic worlds. Our materialized identity, usually called the 'personality aspect', helps us to be grounded in the here and now.

But if we look back at other chapters of this part of our book, we notice that, in effect, we have presented at least four other different spheres of our human identity:

- We started with the aspect of peace as the sound of eternity within our inner self. It can be understood as the face of our identity through which we take permanent part in the cosmic infinity— whether we are aware or not.

- Our soul aspect was presented as another synchronic reality that permeates our existence—when embodied or in the spirit world.
- The theme of our Personal Elemental Being brought to our awareness the existence of the sphere of our identity, as a being of the Earth and nature, taking part at the elemental consciousness of Gaia.
- Next we considered the sphere of feminine and masculine identity. If manifested as a woman, we said, we exist as a man at the parallel (causal, etheric) level and vice versa.

To further complete our insight into the human being as a cluster of synchronic identities, at least two other spheres should be examined.

The first is the sphere of our identity that connects human beings and the animal kingdom. There is a fraction of humankind that would like to suppress this connection, to make clear that we humans are positioned higher in the evolutionary scale then animals. But as long as we are incarnated upon the manifested Earth we can not deny the animal aspect of our identity. I am not speaking specifically to the shamanic tradition of the 'power animal', though my experience says that the animal that 'gives power' to our lives does represent one of our synchronic identities. I am more referring to my perception of the look of one's face and body constitution and how they might present themselves as the embodiment of a specific animal archetype, including that animal's cosmic consciousness and vital powers. It might be a spider, a fox, or perhaps an elephant. The concept of human identity as a cluster of synchronic spheres allows us to honour and experience this aspect of our identity without the threat of losing our human self.

There is also an interesting aspect of the human soul identity that has to do with identification with a specific personality that has walked the Earth in the past. Certain creative individuals during their embodiment on Earth have traced life paths that exist even today upon the etheric levels as a kind of archetype. The soul, preparing for its incarnation, can choose one of these invisible trails as the direction to follow during its future life, in order to embody the specific qualities that the given personality has imprinted while walking upon the Earth. As a result, when finally embodied, this soul walks the course of its life —or a part of it—in synchronicity with Saint Brigit, for example, or King Arthur which in this case represents one of its parallel identities.

The view of a person as a cluster of parallel identities does not lead towards schizophrenia if the human-self understands the present need of accepting multidimensionality as part of their human identity, as an aspect of the ongoing cosmic changes. It is the task of the awakened individual-self to become aware of its synchronic identities and permeate them with its consciousness, love, and creative efforts; making them grounded, interconnected, and active.

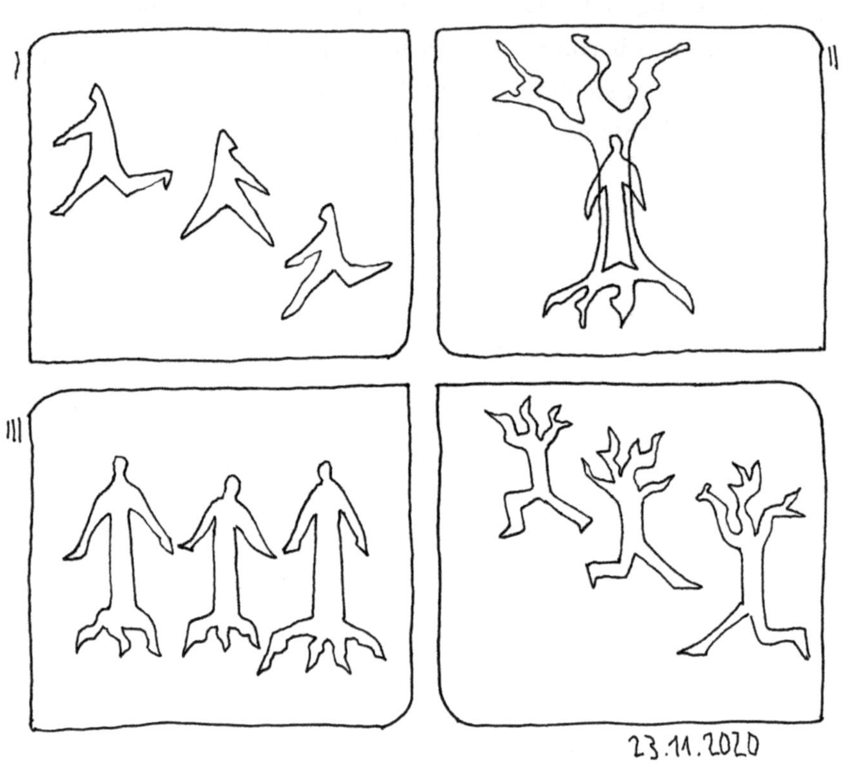

23.11.2020

EXERCISES 2

With Gaia messages

23.11.2020

Human beings, let us be there for each other.
With ever growing awareness,
keep our connectedness alive within you,
for this cycle
of collective transformation.
(Gaia)

- We humans are only used to living amongst our own kind. We consider everything else around us as our environment. This false pattern separates us from the life of Gaia and must be transformed.
- Turn the picture around!
- Imagine you are a tree, firmly rooted in the earth. Notice the trees in your near and far surroundings have become mobile.
- They move around happily while the people all stand rooted to their spots, motionless.
- It is not enough to visualize the inversion; go into the image, let it emerge within you; feel the transformation that happens in you.

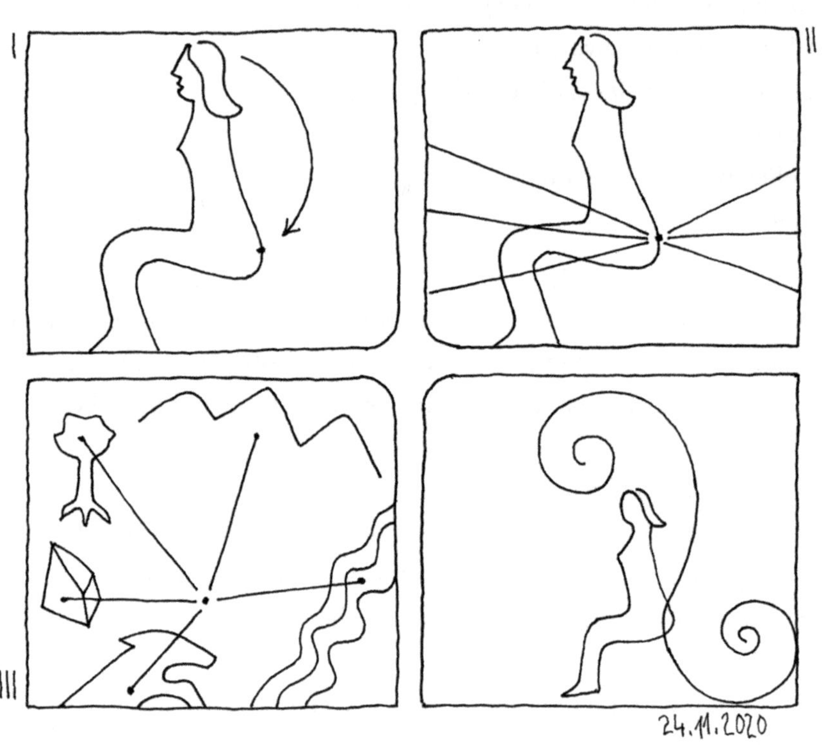

24.11.2020

24.11.2020

Human being, let me communicate with you still.
Stay in touch.
Empower yourself to enliven your spiritual potential,
its inherent creator-wealth,
and thus, prevent separation and division
between one's own interior and the supposed outer.
We are One—keep believing.
Christ in you.
(Gaia)

- Direct your awareness to the point where the tailbone joins the rest of your spine.
- Imagine that countless silver threads emanate from here, connecting you with the surrounding trees, stones, rivers, landscapes, and mountains.
- Feel yourself plugged into this network for a while.
- The trees, stones, rivers, landscapes, and mountains are always and permanently connected to the core of Gaia.
- This secures your reconnection with Gaia. Feel the connection running along your spine and rising up high above your head.
- Then trace the same path back down your spine to the starting point of the exercise.
- Start again from the beginning until you feel firmly anchored in Gaia.

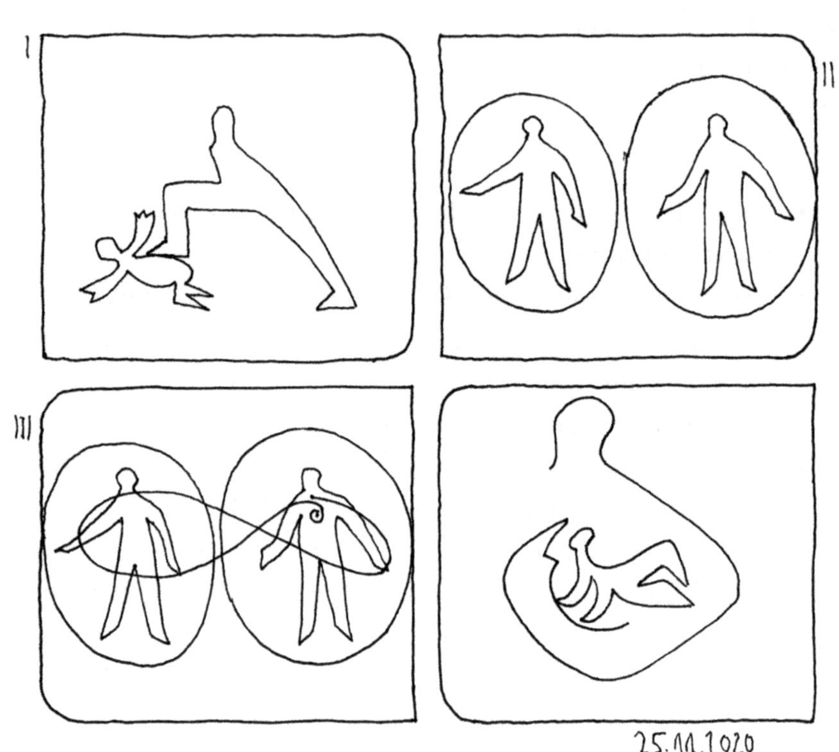

25.11.2020

25.11.2020

Human being—you think what you see is:
Here I am and there are the others.
From the perspective of the connection
with your heart,
the illusion of separation immediately dissolves,
and the possibility of peaceful coexistence becomes apparent.
True peace begins in you.
Christ in you.
(Michael)

- Find your inner peace by being present in the centre of your heart.
- If you look around, you will see countless people pursuing their shallow paths in life and not experiencing inner peace.
- The tragedy is that they drag their accompanying elemental beings into the vortex of their alienation.
- Become aware that although we are operating in two distinct spheres, we all belong to the same human family.
- The elementals belong to the same family of Gaia as your Personal Elemental Being.
- Imagine a lemniscate originating in your heart space that is capable of bridging the gap between us and inspiring our fellow human beings to listen within, to cultivate inner peace and to take one's Personal Elemental Being to heart.

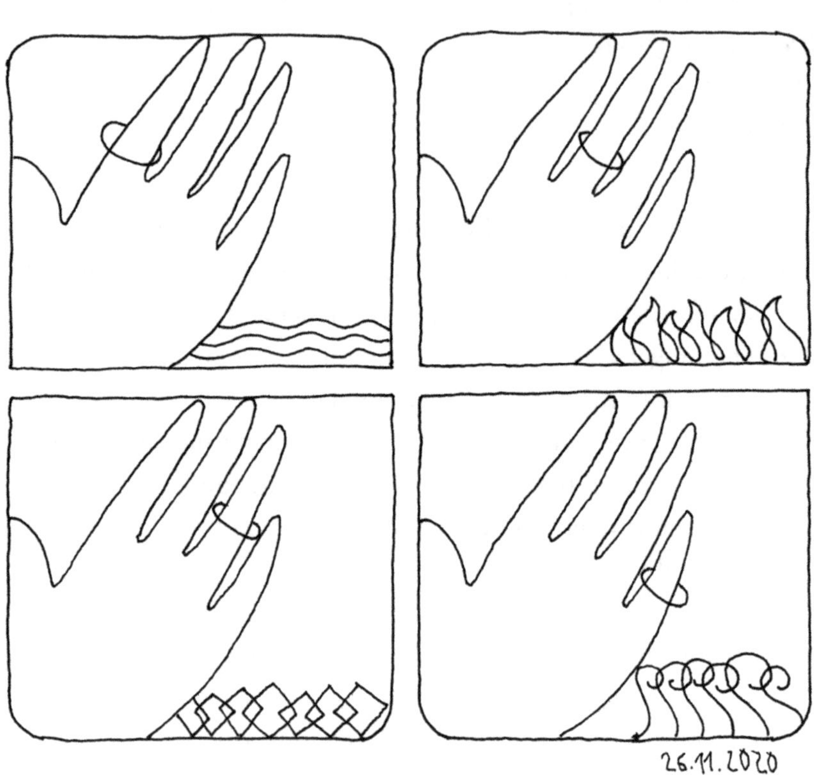

26.11.2020

26.11.2020

Human being—if you are able
to re-entrust yourself ever more to our common space,
you will awaken your creativity.
The inner wealth
which reveals itself to you—here in our togetherness—
makes you stronger and you become healthy in body, mind and soul.
Participate, and continue to do so.
We are ready for the common path.
(Gaia and her beings)

- Imagine a golden ring around the lower tip of your sternum.
- If you put the golden ring on the index finger of your left or right hand, you can perceive the dance of the water element and its beings within you.
- Take time to feel their dance and to dance along with them based on your feelings.
- When you put the golden ring on your middle finger, you can perceive the dance of the element of fire and its transformational beings within you.
- Take time to feel their dance and dance along based on your feelings.
- If you put the golden ring on your ring finger, you can perceive the dance of the earth element and its beings of the mineral kingdom within you.
- Take time to feel their dance and dance along based on your feelings.
- When you put the golden ring on your little finger, you can perceive the dance of the air element and its beings of the earth consciousness within you.
- Take time to feel their dance and dance along based on your feelings.
- Enjoy your renewed relationship with Gaia and her beings!

I
II
III
27.11.2020

27.11.2020

Gratitude and humility
allow you, humans,
to recognize the value of our connectedness.
Thus, our shared path of transformation
into a peaceful coexistence
becomes a reality in the now.
The illusion of separation is dissolving more and more.
We are One—
human beings, continue to recognize the flow of this time,
'Truthfulness'.
(Gaia)

- Become aware that there is a window in your chest through which it is possible to look into the etheric spaces of the causal world, where entities and forces reside that make life in the embodied plane possible.
- But your window is dirty, because in the course of the last centuries most have forgotten that human beings can look into the loving face of the Mother of the earthly paradise through this inner window.
- Now decide to clean your window.
- Imagine making clockwise circular movements with one hand on the front of your windowpane.
- Then switch hands and imagine cleaning the back of the window in a counter-clockwise circular motion.
- Now look through the clean window and enjoy the renewed relationship with the origins of life.

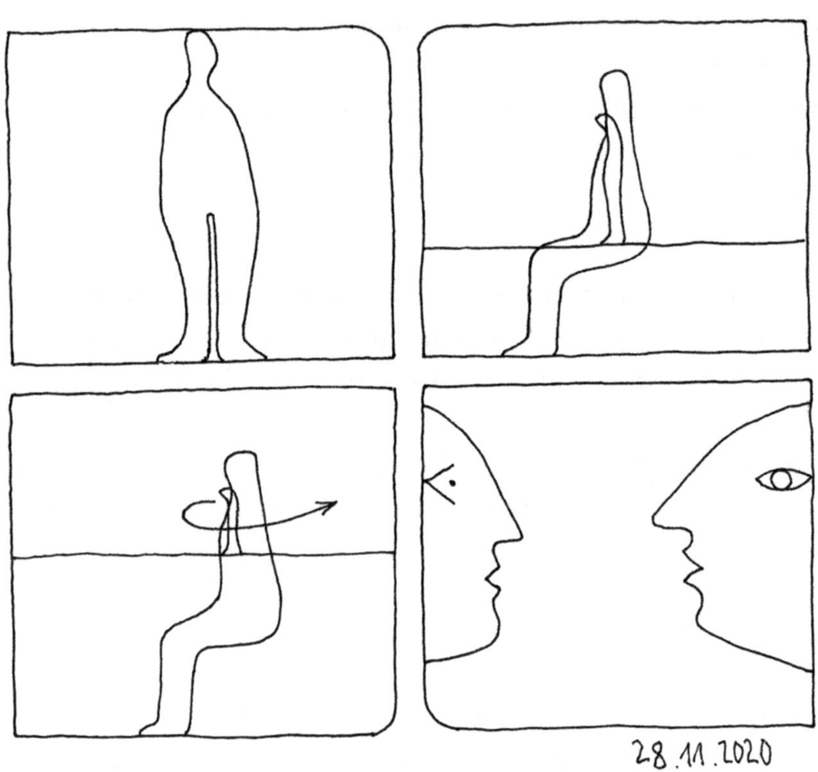

28.11.2020

28.11.2020

Human being—join me.
Enter time and again our common spiritual space.
The more deliberately you seek our association,
the clearer our shared creative space will reveal itself to you.
Here with me, you will become aware of your potential for this earthly
path.
(Gaia)

- The exercise begins in a standing position.
- Feel your presence from the soles of your feet to the top of your skull.
- Now sit down and remain seated for the rest of the exercise.
- Imagine you are standing at the level of your tailbone and that the top of your head is level with the top of your skull. Now you are smaller, but more concentrated in your power. Feel it.
- Then take the next step upwards.
- Now you are standing at the level of the lower tip of the sternum, with your head still reaching up to the top of the skull.
- How does it feel to stand at the level of your Personal Elemental Being and to be as small as a child?
- Now imagine turning around towards your back space and look into the eyes of Gaia. Your eyes are now at the same level.
- Use this closeness to Gaia to connect more deeply with her.
- Then, rising, step back onto terra firma to embody the experience.

29.11.2020

29.11.2020

Human being—
your engagement with me,
your belief and trust
in the elemental worlds
facilitates the journey
into your creative potential.
(Gaia)

- Imagine the globe of the Earth as so small that you can sit on it comfortably. Make sure to sit on a continent so your bottom stays dry.
- Stretch your legs into the water of the nearby ocean.
- Feel the power of life rising up your spine, nourishing you with the wisdom and love of Gaia.
- Notice how the power of her dragons supports you in every situation of your life.
- Finally, get up and stand up to your ankles in the ocean's water; give thanks for these gifts.

30.11.2020

30.11.2020

Human beings—let yourselves again be touched
by the elemental realms;
embrace our invitation.
Return to the connectedness,
to live it—from now on,
in our renewed alliance, which is presently coming into being.
(Gaia and her beings)

- Imagine the sun so high above you that it cannot be seen.
- You can however feel the sun's love and warmth. This causes all the connections between the cells and between the microbes of your body to be thawed, giving way to a unique openness to transformation within your body.
- Now the gravitational pull of the moon begins its work. It has the power of creating the high and low tides of the oceans.
- The magnetic pull of the moon is extracting toxins and dead intercellular connections from your body that will be stored in the mineral layers of the moon for recycling.
- Now the wisdom of Gaia comes into play.
- Her elementals fill the emptied micro-spaces in your body with the golden essence of her wisdom.
- Feel yourself renewed and reconnected with Gaia and her beings.

PART 3: APOCALYPSE AS A MATRIX OF THE FUTURE CULTURE

The seed of Gaia Culture

The events after the year zero (when our counting of years began) have left a strong imprint upon the destiny of humankind. They have caused the flow of human evolution and the evolution of the Earthly cluster to turn in a new direction. One could argue that this applies only to the Western world. But, can the Earth be divided into East and West? *Can the global civilization of today be divided into East and West?*

Around the year 30 AD. Jesus from Nazareth—later called the Christ—started his three years' cycle of public teaching and healing. In the midst of an extreme patriarchal society, he formulated a completely new ethical codex of human relationships towards fellow human beings and Divinity. Unfortunately he didn't leave behind any documents concerning his original teaching, so it was easy in the following centuries to adapt his teachings to the needs of the Christian church, a rapidly growing religious institution. My book *Christ Power and Earth Wisdom* explores distortions of Jesus' teaching, as formulated in the four canonical Gospels that represent the foundation of Christian churches.

About 60 years later, one of his disciples, John, who knew Jesus as a young man, had to flee from persecution to the Greek island of Patmos where he wrote a book listening to his inner voice. The book, preserved in the official Christian Bible as the last of its chapters, is called the Apocalypse. Translated, 'Apocalypse' means to take the lid off the vessel (containing the future events). In this sense, it is also called the 'Revelation of Saint John'. We will use both names, the Apocalypse and the Revelation, interchangeably.

In the present book we follow the paths leading towards a new Gaia-related culture. Why waste time on two-millennia-old Scripture? It is for the benefit of our intent. My insight says that the cosmic purpose behind writing the Apocalypse was to create a seed for the transformation and transmutation of our home planet and human culture, predicted to germinate at the threshold of the third millennium. So diving into the Apocalypse, we can touch upon the foundations of the culture called Gaia Culture.

Given the organic cycle of growth, it is impossible to imagine that our generation could arrive at the threshold of the third millennium and successfully start a new culture from nothing. The seed of today's developing culture would had to have been formed and planted almost two thousand years ago, allowing it time in Gaia's womb, to enable germination at the threshold of the third millennium.

We are not interested in delivering another, among many attempts to decode the secret language of the Apocalypse. We will try to present the Apocalypse as a guide to the matrix of (future) Gaia Culture by comparing the course of the Earth's transformation process during the last two decades with the information stored in the Revelation of Saint John. Secondly—and this is the main purpose of this examination—we will try to learn from the Apocalypse as much as possible about the original inspiration that pushed forward the creation of a new more holistic human culture on Earth.

It would certainly not be possible to use the Apocalypse as a guide, if the message written had not been protected and pure. Over the centuries many of the Scriptures have been altered and adapted to the will of the Christian church to maintain power and control over future events. The protection of the message in Revelation is found in the double structure of the book. On one hand, it is written so that it can be read from the beginning to end. The usual interpretations are based on this linear approach. Such a path is useful to the logical mind, but it leaves the investigator lost among a flood of symbols and repeating images.

Preparing my book *Earth Changes, Human Destiny*, where I compare the Earth-transforming process with the Revelation of Saint John, I was made aware by my elemental master that there is another way to read Revelation. The seed of the future Gaia Culture is hidden in a concentric reading of the Apocalypse. One should start to read at the centre of the book—Chapter 12—and then read a chapter to the right and afterwards a chapter to the left and so on. Like rings, the chapters are composed around the centre. The book ends with the first and the last chapters, whose subject matter is closely related.

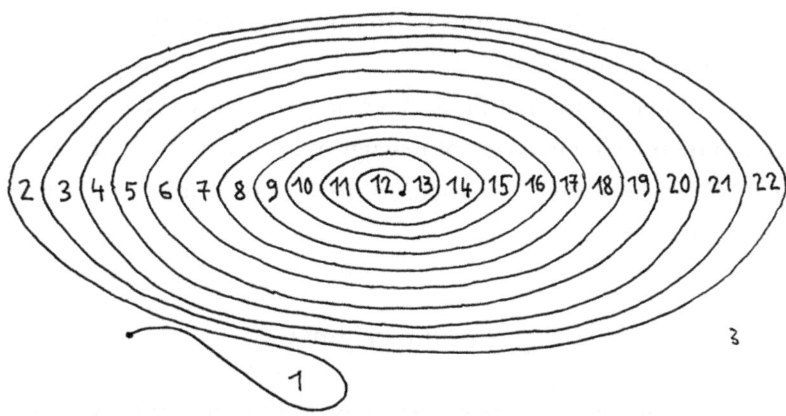

The concentric composition of the Apocalypse vs its linear

Before we dive into exploring the messages of the Apocalypse I would like to make three remarks:

First, be aware that the Apocalypse was written in a time when it was believed that the teaching of Jesus the Christ represented an effort to renew the Jewish religion—not representing a revolutionary change in relationship to the sacred dimensions of life on Earth and to Divinity. As a result, the Apocalypse is heavily overlaid with the monotheistic patterns originating in the Jewish and remodelled by the Christian culture. I will try and navigate through the Revelation of Saint John so as to avoid ballast that only confuses its message for the future of Earth and humankind.

Second, during the last two millennia, the Apocalypse was often used to make people fear the so-called 'Last Judgement'—when Divinity would arrive to separate good people from bad ones, throwing the last ones into Hell. I need to make clear at this point that the dualistic pattern of dividing by cursing one side and celebrating the other is not acceptable from the point of view of the Earthly cosmos. This form of harsh judgement has no place in a culture of learning and developing, composed of diverse beings and evolutions, working in the name of freedom, and with a loving attitude toward all.

The third remark relates to the expression 'apocalyptic', often used to denote events in human and Earth's history, seeming to project the destruction of humankind.

We should be aware that these three negative patterns are purposely used to hide the true message of Revelation, dedicated to our common future. We should not allow them to distract us from our purpose of exploring the Apocalypse.

Cosmic origins

One of the most precious messages delivered by the Apocalypse is the affirmation that developing Gaia Culture upon the Earth is not just a local project for our galaxy. It has cosmic dimensions and can be seen as an initiation to open an important door for the whole universe as it expands to a completely new phase of its evolution.

Consider the following; all efforts of modern science to find other traces of life in our galactic environment have been in vain. There are none. The universe may burst with life at different more subtle levels of existence, it may have marvellous civilizations in different star systems, but it does not know spiritual life embodied in matter, as the Earth knows it.

This conviction is based upon my interpretation of the central 12th chapter of the Apocalypse. It starts with the words: 'Then a huge sign became visible in the sky—the figure of a woman clothed with the sun, with the moon under her feet, and a crown of twelve stars upon her head.' (Rev. 12:1-2). At its central point, the Apocalypse confronts us with the revelation of the new feminine dimension of the universe, positioned with the cosmic context of Moon, Sun, and stars; asserting a unique cosmic event.

The first sentence of the central chapter of the Apocalypse confirms the inverted proportion between the feminine and masculine principles, as explored in one of our previous chapters. At the central point of creation, where past patriarchal bias should dictate the appearance of a male God, the Apocalypse enthrones a woman, as the future axis around which the universe should evolve in the ages ahead.

Revelation continues by declaring her pregnant with 'a male child, who is to shepherd all the nations with a rod of iron'. As already stated previously in relationship to the present Earth Changes, the feminine principle (the cosmic Yin) becomes the leading impetus of future evolution. Its masculine counterpart should enter a process of retreat from its dominant position in human culture, to be reborn as the new partner of the 'Woman in the sky', but not with the golden sceptre in the hand as the ruling principle, but as co-creator 'with the iron rod'. Iron, as deference to gold, is understood as a symbol of 'active doing' as opposed to 'leading'.

But the vision of the 'Woman in the sky' represents only one half of the central chapter of Revelation. It is intertwined with 'another sign visible in the sky'. John saw it as an equally huge 'red dragon with seven heads and ten horns, with a diadem upon each of his heads, his tail sweeping down a third of the stars in the sky...' (Rev. 12:3-4)

I am sorry that the symbol of dragon is used in this image. From my experience, I know dragons as primeval powers of creation, at levels of the Earth or of the universe. In the absence of a more proper word, we have to accept the 'red dragon' with seven crowned heads as representing the old ruling principle of the universe that is in process of stepping back. The cosmic time has arrived to give his place at the centre of the cosmos freely to the 'Woman in the sky'. The Apocalypse confirms our notion expressed previously, that in facing the new age of universal development, the hierarchically organized masculine ruling power has to retreat and subdue to the cycle of the cosmic change.

We are next shown that the cosmic masculine power is not ready to undergo a transmutation process, or let go its ruling position: 'The dragon took his place in front of the woman who was about to give birth to a child, so that as soon as she did so he might devour it.' (Rev. 12:5)

Using its symbolic language, the Apocalypse shows us that the universe enters a similar epochal change, simultaneously with the Earth's transformation process (as described in the Introduction). We have two parallel processes at two different levels. In both cases the change in the universal cycle demands that the hierarchical male principle retreats, to give its place to the feminine matrix, based upon horizontal heart-to-heart relationships between different worlds and beings.

What is equally important for us is the information that the cosmic masculine, on rejecting the process of change, takes on the role of the counter-force against the New. As such it is forced to leave the already transformed and renewed universe, being expelled to the Earth: 'So the huge dragon, the serpent of the ancient times… was hurled down upon the Earth, and his angels were hurled down with him.' (Rev. 12:9)

This statement makes it clear that what is presently transpiring on Earth is an important part of the cosmic drama. The new cosmic order has been established in the universe, while the old hierarchical principle—opposing the change—has been expelled to the Earth. Why? Does the Earth represent a cosmic recycling station? The answer may be found in the words that accompany the expelling of the counter-force to the Earth: 'Therefore, rejoice, O Heavens and all you who live in the Heavens! But alas for the Earth and the Sea, for the devil has come down to you in great fury, knowing that his time is short.' (Rev. 12:12)

I wish to point to the expression 'knowing that his time is short'. Revelation makes it clear that the cosmic drama of change in the rest of the universe is already concluded while its last sequence needs to be fought out upon the Earth. If the Earth were destined to become a cosmic recycling place, no time limit would be set to the presence of cosmic counter-force on our home planet.

Why then must the last sequence of the cosmic drama happen on Earth? Even if it is a heavy burden for Gaia, it must be fought upon the Earth, because it is Gaia's planet that stepped forward to pioneer the new path of the universal evolution. Gaia, evolving her creation throughout millions of years, has succeeded in settling life at the embodied level, be it microorganisms, plants, animals, dolphins, human beings etc. Even highly evolved and conscious forms of culture, for example, the ancient Chinese, Egyptian, or Mayan, were given the advantage of developing in the condition of matter, a fantastic achievement of Gaia in cooperation with humankind. She enables the invisible spiritual dimensions to express through matter.

Creating the seed of the multidimensional Gaia Culture is the next step.

If successful, then the evolution of the universe and its worlds could manifest deeper, making it possible for cultures to manifest at a more grounded, direct, heart-to-heart level. This is the reason why the counter-forces work so hard to preserve the old hierarchical universe. Gaia's heart-to-heart culture would make it very difficult to pit one culture or group against another. Gaia's work is to first prove consistency of the new path, before it can become the universal quality.

Counter-force to the New

Now we leave behind the central 12th chapter of Revelation to start our move through the ten rings that surround it. The first ring is composed of the 13th chapter at the right side of the book and the 11th at the left. They both deliver information important to us about the circumstances within which the emergence of the new Gaia Culture evolves. Together they reveal the widely hidden truth of events on Earth and among humankind after the cosmic counter-force descended and established itself upon the planet.

We are shown that after stepping down from the cosmic level, 'the red dragon' took the form of two complementary forces called 'beasts'. One manifested in the Element-Water and the other in the Element-Earth. The intent of the watery 'beast' is to detach people from their natural connectedness to Gaia and from the spiritual essence of being human. With the words of Saint John: '…there rose out of the sea before my eyes a beast with seven heads and ten horns… and blasphemous names upon its horns… the whole [humanity] followed the beast with wonder… (Rev. 13:1-4)

I need to explain my exchanging of the word 'earth' with 'humanity', in the above quotation. It was done so as to make clear that the only beings of the Earth taken in by the 'beast' were human. All other beings of Earth were not followers, but victims of human blindness. As in the case of the use of the word 'dragon', these misrepresentations are attributable to the loss of geomantic knowledge from Earth during the time Revelation was written. In my edition of the Bible, the two 'beasts' were called 'animals'; also unacceptable.

Continuing to characterize the first beast, the Apocalypse says: 'Moreover it was permitted to make war upon the saints and to conquer them; the authority given to it extended over every tribe and people and language and nation.' (Rev. 13:8) Translated, its task was to work on the psychic level to make people of the Earth follow false ideologies, ungrounded religious visions, one-sided scientific ideas, political utopia etc.

The beast that John described rising out of the Earth, would lead people astray with the help of technological wonders: 'It performs great signs: before men's eyes it makes fire fall down from Heaven to the Earth… Further it was allowed to give breath of life to the statue of the [first] beast so that the statue could speak and condemn to death all those who do not worship its statue.' (Rev. 13:13-15)

At that time there could be no knowledge of our rockets shot to the sky and falling back to the Earth, also no idea about robots, presented as a 'speaking statue'. We can even find an allusion of the dangerous genetic engineering: 'Then it compels all, small and great, rich and poor… to receive a mark on their right hands or on their foreheads. The purpose of this is that no one should be able to buy or to sell unless he bears the mark of the name of the beast or the number of its name.' (Rev. 13:16-18) Translated, it means that the beast brings to Earth the danger of the coupling of electronic media with the human being—the total control of society and its members.

The Apocalypse also reveals a secret related to the two beasts. They not only exist outside of us—directly influencing humankind, but have succeeded (probably with the help of genetic engineering) to break into the causal dimensions of humankind to simultaneously abide within our psyche and consciousness, pushing human individuals and nations from inside to perform actions that work against the human matrix. This sad assertion is hidden in the often referred to number 666: 'Understanding is needed here: Let every thinking man calculate the number of the beast. It is the number of a man, and its number is six hundred and sixty six.' (Rev. 13:18)

Note: 'Man' is the old expression for the human being, derived from the ages when the existence of women seemed unimportant to the 'glorious history of mankind'. In this sense the above quotation can be understood as predicting that the counter-force will find ways to sneak inside the human essence to become an influential parasite.

Support from Heaven

As we continue to unpeel the onion of the Apocalypse, we will see that the incarnation of contrary forces to the new cycle of Gaia's evolution is not the only 'gift' of the universe to Earth and humankind. Chapter 11, positioned at the opposite side of the central 12th chapter, testifies to enlightened beings sent to Earth and humanity from the universe to help us meet the challenges of the above-described cosmic drama.

Two witnesses of Divinity are sent to the Earth, to 'measure its temple'. I understand this expression as a message about measuring the sacred dimensions of our home planet. John wrote down the following word of Divinity: 'And I will give authority to my two witnesses to proclaim the message, clothed in sackcloth for twelve hundred and sixty days.' Do not think me crazy if I believe this refers to Gautama

Buddha in the East and Jesus Christ in the West. Their teachings had the weight of divine messaging for humanity, that were transformed into, more or less, formalized religions.

The Apocalypse proclaims that the counter-forces will act severely to undermine the tasks of the two witnesses, in order to prevent people of Earth from being inspired by their example and: 'Then, when their work of witnesses is complete, the beast will come out of its pit and go to war with them. It will conquer and kill them, and their bodies will lie in the street of the great city… For three and a half days some from all peoples and tribes and languages and nations will gaze upon their bodies and will not allow them to be buried.' (Rev. 11:9-10)

One side of Chapter 11 testifies to the disastrous traces left in the psyche of humanity by the counter-forces within the last three millennia. I mark three millennia as starting around 1000 BC., the masculine-governed age, historically called the 'Iron Age', when melting iron was invented. This age is notorious for merciless wars and general loss of compassion towards beings of nature and fellow human beings—unfortunately, still the general characteristic of present-day human civilization.

On the other side, the 11th chapter brings hope, asserting that humankind is not left alone while struggling with forces that want to close the door to the New. The words of the Apocalypse honour those countless individuals, usually called 'saints', that again and again take upon themselves the challenges of their incarnation to bring hope to fellow human beings, to initiate ethical values in relationships between human individuals and nations, and to demonstrate the existence of divine dimensions of existence. In this sense, Revelation continues: 'But after three and half days the Spirit of life from God entered them and they stood upright on their feet. This struck terror into the hearts of those who were watching them, and they heard a tremendous voice speaking to those two from Heaven, saying: Come up here!' (Rev. 11:11-12)

The Seven Seals

Chapters 5 through 8, dedicated to the famous Seven Seals of the Apocalypse, are positioned left of the central 12th chapter. They are especially interesting for our exploration of Gaia-Culture background because they deal with seven paths along which the formation of the new Earth and the new humanity shall evolve.

The story begins with the book of future events, sealed with seven seals. John writes: 'And I saw a mighty angel who called out in a loud voice: Who is fit to open the book and break its seals? And no one in Heaven or upon Earth or under the Earth was able to open the book or even look at it. I began to weep bitterly because no one could be found fit to open the book… (Rev. 5:2-5)

The one fit to break the seals and open the book appeared as a lamb with seven horns and seven eyes. This is certainly a surprise, that an animal could do what was impossible even for the highest beings of the spiritual worlds! You may be even more surprised if I identify the lamb as Pan, whom we know as the ancient Greek god of nature.

I dared to identify the lamb as 'Pan' after a vision of Pan appeared to me, in gigantic stature, in Saarland, Germany on 27 May, 2000. He raised his mighty arms and I could clearly see wounds on his hands, his feet and, at his right side, what is known as stigmata—the marks of Christ's presence. Stigmata represent the spiritual imprints of the five wounds that were inflicted upon Jesus (later called the Christ), during his sacrifice on the cross. I must add, Western tradition identifies Christ as carrier of the 'cosmic inspiration' (from the Apocalypse, Chapter 12) to the Earth and its beings, including to Gaia and Pan.

Pan can be considered the masculine aspect of Gaia. Gaia permanently creates conditions for life, projecting them from the Earth's core towards the surface of the planet. Pan cares for all manifested life-forms inhabiting Earth.

The Greek iconography shows Pan as a goat god. In Christian symbolism, the goat represents the shadow side of the human being, while the lamb represents the positive aspect—open to the future. Contrarily, the Apocalypse shows Pan in the form of a lamb and not as a goat. Yet to make clear that Pan, and all nature of the Earth that he represents, was touched by the presence of Christ, the Apocalypse shows him with the signs of his transformation—seven horns and seven eyes.

What is also important to realize for our investigation, is that to open the Book of future events required a *divine being belonging to the Earthly cosmos.*

The process of future Gaia Culture starts with the words of Saint John: 'Then I watched when the lamb broke the first of the Seven Seals… and before my eyes was a white horse. Its rider carried a bow, and he was given a crown.' (Rev. 6:1-2)

The rider on the white horse represents the basic change in the cosmic cycle, transitioning to the New possibility. The Element-Earth ruled the previous (and mostly, still the present) development of the Earth. This is the reason we still find ourselves today in an ambience of matter. The new incoming cycle is the one of the Element-Air, expressed by the first apocalyptic rider carrying a bow, a tool for sending messages through the air. Element-Air, unlike the hard matter of Element-Earth, supports consciousness as the ruling principle of future evolution—a crowned ruler, riding a white horse.

Element-Air is the element of freedom at all levels of existence. The crown denotes this role of the Element-Air among the four Elements. It is the Element that completes the grand cycle of development of Gaia that started billions of years ago with the subtle planet ruled by the Element-Fire. Evolution continued from Fire to the dilution of the Earth with the Element-Water, succeeded by the present Element-Earth. The future era governed by the Element-Air, offers possibilities for creating the Gaia Culture and, by this 'crowning', planetary evolution—the highest possible achievement. (For more information look into my book, *Dancing with the Earth Changes.*)

'Then when the lamb broke the second seal another horse came forth, red in colour. Its rider was given power to deprive the Earth of peace, so that men should kill each other. A huge sword was put into his hand.' (Rev. 6:2-4)

With the red horse and the sword, we are shown the second aspect of development leading towards Gaia Culture. It will not be a peaceful path, but a path of constant changes, some of which might be rather painful. The reason is that the archetypes (matrix) both of Gaia and humankind have peculiarities that make the transformation processes complicated.

Gaia has the special gift to enable developing and upholding life in embodied form, which is not so easy to change, especially when the life is embodied in matter. This may cause changes that are far from peaceful.

As human beings, we are proud holders of the gift of free will. In other words, nobody on Earth or in the Heavens can push us to do something that we do not want to do. Unfortunately, this unique cosmic gift is massively misused due to different forms of egocentrism, making the processes of change even more difficult. Since the cosmic clock moves at its own rhythm, it often means that the individual human's will-to-obstruct must be broken. Forcing the necessary changes will then result in dramatic consequences for individuals or humanity as a whole.

'When the lamb broke the third seal… before my eyes was a black horse. Its rider had a pair of scales in his hand, and I heard a voice… saying: a quart of wheat for a shilling, and three quarts of barley for a shilling—but no tampering with the oil or the wine!' (Rev. 6:5-6)

The symbol of scales shows us a balancing of opposites. Wheat and barley as dry substances represent the Yang aspect of balance, whilst oil and wine represent the fluid Yin.

Translated into logical language, and supported by my experiences with geomantic work after the year 1998, I can testify to a drastic shifting of planetary balances. I have included my drawings, showing the configuration of etheric masses of the four Elements in my country Slovenia, before and after the solar eclipse of 11 August, 1999.

There are four foci of the four Elements, each in a fixed spot in the landscape of Slovenia. Each was separately supplied with life-force. After the solar eclipse, the clouds of the Elemental life powers showed a much more clear, almost symmetrical pattern, centred on the fifth Element cupola positioned at the country's centre, marked with its capital Ljubljana. The pattern of their balances might be nowadays again different.

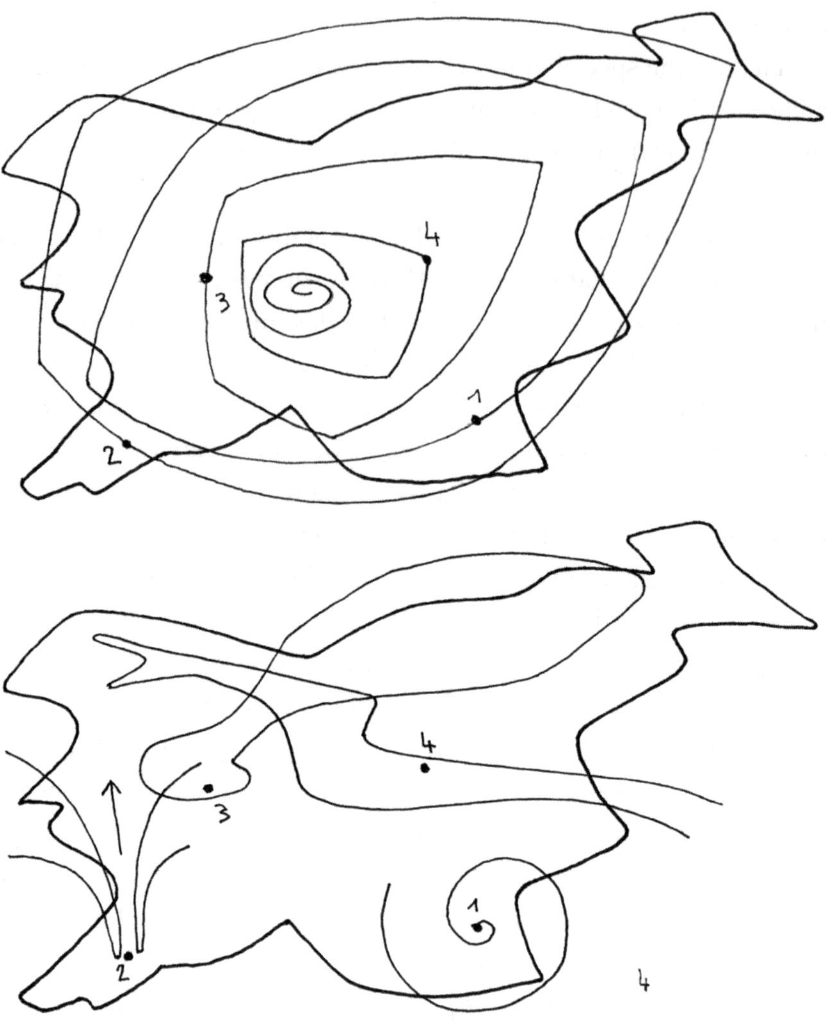

The etheric configuration of my country Slovenia before (below) and after (above) the solar eclipse of 11 August, 1999. The borders of the country are marked with the thicker line. The numbers denote foci of one of the four Elements.

'Then when he broke the fourth seal… there appeared a horse sickly green in colour. The name of its rider was death and the grave followed close behind him.' (Rev. 6:7-8)

The fourth seal was difficult to crack for me because of the innate human fear of death I share with humanity. Luckily, while writing the earlier mentioned book, *Earth Changes and Human Destiny*, I had the chance to talk to my elemental master, Julius. He suggested connecting the idea of death with the phrase 'the grave followed close behind him'. The grave, representing the moment when one leaves the physical world behind while entering the spiritual dimensions, should be understood as an inter-dimensional portal leading from one dimension of existence into another.

The symbol of death can be understood as a movement through an inter-dimensional portal to connect with parallel worlds. The fourth seal shows us that Gaia Culture will open portals to parallel worlds, generally closed to embodied human beings. In the past, only chosen people like shamans, oracles, and some priests knew how to enter the parallel worlds—elemental, sub-elemental, faery, or angelic. With the development of Gaia Culture, exchange between different extensions of the Earthly cosmos should become a common heritage.

Now we have arrived at the fifth seal, which reveals a crowd of human beings in white robes. This seal relates to the processes and the relationship of humankind to the matrix of being human, and the acknowledgment of the cosmic task before us.

The first part of the text of the fifth seal seems rather confusing: 'How long shall it be, O Lord of all holy and true, before thou shalt judge and avenge our blood upon the inhabitants of the Earth?' (Rev. 6:10)

My intuition says that the human beings in white robes who speak this plea are original human souls, belonging to the evolution of the human race. The other crowd of souls that 'shed their blood upon the inhabitants of the Earth' could be called 'tourist' souls that have infiltrated the human family to experience and enjoy the extraordinary manifested world of the Earth's landscapes. Like crowds of tourists visiting Stonehenge, Venice, or the Great Pyramid, they took advantage by using the gateway of birth to appear in a human body.

The problem is that they are neither attuned to the matrix of Gaia, nor to the archetype of the human family. So they behave destructively, in the ecological sense, as well as pushing humanity into suicidal situations, like those of international conflicts and wars. How could it come about that they arrived in such crowds upon the Earth? I am sure that this is the strategy of the counter-forces presented in the 13th chapter. They used the human loss of identity to cause a loss of control over the birth process. Due to human free will, neither Gaia nor responsible spiritual masters could prevent it.

The Apocalypse predicts as part of the Earth Changes a process of division through which the original human souls will be recognized as such by 'clothing them into white robes'. Those who have no cosmic right to walk upon the Earth will have to return to their home star systems and planets—but they do have a valid reason to take part in the future Gaia Culture. So the Apocalypse asks the human family to be patient. This process should not be done by shedding blood: 'Then each of them was given a white robe, and they were told to be patient a little longer until the number of their fellow servants and of their brethren, who were to die as they had died, should be complete.' (Rev. 6:11); meaning the mentioned division should be made through the path of natural death.

Opening the sixth seal can be understood as predicting changes at the subtle and physical levels of the planetary space: 'Then I watched while he broke the sixth seal. There was a tremendous earthquake, the sun turned dark like coarse black cloth, and the full moon was red as blood. The stars of the sky fell upon the earth, just as a fig tree sheds unripe figs when shaken in a gale. The sky vanished as though it were a scroll being rolled up, and every mountain and island was jolted out of its place.' (Rev. 6:12-14)

The sixth seal talks about the gradual transformation of the three-dimensional space of the Earth into a multidimensional one. It gives clear notice that this is a demanding process that might at moments look as if the Earth is falling apart. The image of the scroll is an important symbol denoting the change from a linear to a spherical space structure. The sky is not only above the Earth, but will be perceived within the Earth simultaneously, rolled together like a scroll of paper. Stars, with their civilizations that seem many light years away from us, may become our close neighbours at another level of existence—as stated above in relationship to the stars fallen upon the Earth.

The sixth seal predicts also that the geographical configuration may change drastically in the following centuries, probably as the cause of a gradual pole shift. But there is no reason for panic, if the breaking of the sixth seal is understood as proceeding simultaneously with the other five seals. The other five seals let us know that the Earth is preparing parallel realities, and also interdimensional portals, through which it is possible to reach them. So Gaia can move the sphere of life, with humankind included, to safe places— to some safe vital-energy levels—for the time being, for the events upon the manifested Earth may otherwise ruin the network of life and its beings.

The opening of the seventh seal was followed by seven angels sounding Seven trumpets: 'The first angel blew their trumpet. Hail and fire mingled with blood appeared and were hurled upon the Earth. One third of the Earth was burned up...' (Rev. 8:7)

The Seven trumpets, and traumatic events they call into existence, symbolize the difficult psychic conditions that peoples of Earth must endure as they hold fast to the old image of Earth that, in effect, no longer exists. It only exists, against the law of the cosmic cycle, because millions of people still hold it in their unconscious imagination, acting as if it still exists. Humankind thus calls these troubles upon themselves! Those called into existence by the sound of the Seven trumpets should help us to detach from the old and open for the New.

The horrible events, presented as blasé, of the Seven trumpets, come indeed one after the other upon us: the fall of the twin towers in New

York; hurricanes stronger then ever; earthquakes; the burning of Notre Dame Cathedral in Paris; months of fires in the woods of Australia; the explosion of the Fukushima atomic plant; the rising of the sea level which pushes millions of people to migrate; the Covid-19 pandemic with the global lockdown ruining the world economy and giving rise to autocratic regimes etc.

As stated already, one should hold fast to the conviction that all the seven lines of the epochal Earth Changes written in the Book with the Seven Seals run parallel to each other, intertwining, separating and connecting again… Some of them, if taken separately from each other, could have devastating effects upon the Earth and its living beings. But all together, they carry the potential to accomplish the manifestation of the new Gaia Culture upon Earth and to fulfil the task that the Earth has in the context of that larger arc of changes that touches the universe as the whole.

Cultural break down

Keeping in mind the spherical composition of the Apocalypse, we should now look to the other side of the central Chapter 12, to the Chapters 16 through 18. They present John's vision of the decay and final breakdown of the old, patriarchal human culture, or simply, the Old age.

Before we look at this unpleasant story, I must again protest! Women are misused to portray the dark sides of a culture, a culture that was clearly created by masculine will and power! Similarly, in the cases of the dragons and animals mentioned above, women were perceived in Revelation (or more likely, its translators) as lower 'material'—thus as a suitable symbol for the negative side of creation.

Chapter 16 describes the outpouring from the seven terrible bowls 'of God's wrath' upon the Earth and its people. It is more or less a repetition of the seven sounds of trumpets from Chapter 8, needed at this point to support the symmetrical composition of the Apocalypse.

One of the angels who poured out the seven bowls spoke to John: 'Come and I will show you the judgement passed upon the great harlot who is seated upon many waters. It is with her that the kings of the Earth have debauched themselves and the inhabitants of the Earth have become drunk on the wine of her filthiness.' (Rev. 17:1-2)

It is logical that the Old culture, built upon mass emotions, personal fears of all kinds, hate of other nations and races, massive distortions of truth, egocentric attitude towards life etc., needs to collapse before the new culture can manifest. As the above words of the angel reveal, positioning the harlot upon 'many waters', the decaying culture is not grounded any more in the essence of Gaia, but is navigated by negative and destructive emotions. Water is the proper symbol for the emotional level—in this case, for the so-called 'lower astral'.

Even though women and the Element-Water are misused in the 17th chapter, I felt it necessary to direct attention to its message, because it shows the hidden causal background of our modern day-to-day destructive planetary culture.

To indicate that we have moved from the manifested to the causal level of the Old culture, John is moved to the desert: 'There I saw a woman riding upon a scarlet beast, covered with blasphemous titles and having seven heads and ten horns. The woman herself was dressed in purple and scarlet, glittering with gold, jewels and pearls.' (Rev. 17:3-4)

What the Apocalypse reveals is the 'red dragon' (the cosmic counter-force), infiltrating itself into the fabric of the last three millennia of human culture, pushing it towards the awful condition in which we find ourselves today. Incarnated as the two beasts (presented in Chapter 13), the cosmic counter-force can reach all different dimensions of human psyche and cultural activity. If we as individual human beings do not detach from its devastating influence, then we become its servants, and ultimately its slaves.

The Apocalypse warns that following the wrong path, the one permeated into human consciousness and activities by the counter-force, can lead us to suicide as a human race. This is the message of the angel's continued explanation: 'As for the waters which you saw, on which the harlot took her seat, they are peoples and vast crowds, nations and languages. The ten horns and the beast that you saw will loathe the harlot, and leave her deserted and naked. Moreover, it will devour her flesh, and then consume her with fire.' (Rev. 17:15-16)

Chapter 18 is a serious warning addressed to humankind to quit the wrong path: 'Then I heard another voice from Heaven, crying: Come out of her, O my people, lest you become accomplices in her sins and must share in her punishment. For her sins have mounted up to the sky, and God has remembered the tale of her wickedness.' (Rev. 18:4-6)

In the following Apocalypse quotation, 'Babylon' represents the old culture; 'New Jerusalem' marks the space of the New culture—in the present book called 'Gaia Culture':

'So shall Babylon, the great city be sent hurling down to disappear forever! Never more shall the sound of harpist and musicians, flute players and trumpeters be heard in you again! Never again shall a craftsman of any craft be found in you; never again will the sound of the mill-stone's grinding be heard in you! No light of a lamp shall ever shine in you again, and the voices of bridegroom and bride shall be heard in you no more! The fruit of your soul's desire is lost to you for ever.' (Rev. 18:21-23) Returning to the manifested level of reality in the year 2020, we hear lamentation of the people of Earth for the, more or less, complete lockdown of human activities: no more concerts, craft and spiritual workshops, air traffic, travel or tourism, restaurants, funerals, weddings, religious services, etc.

Take care; the farewell from the old culture, as described in the story of Babylon—especially in the last quotation—is imbued with hidden hate against the beauty and strength of embodied life, and consequently, against Gaia as its creator. In this sense, Babylon, as the 'great whore', can be seen as a false interpretation from a follower of monotheistic religion, renouncing the importance of the natural world; a characteristic view of early Christianity.

Establishing new ethics

After describing the breakdown of the old culture, we follow the Apocalypse back to the beginning of the Book, to Chapters 2 through 3.

Here are found encrypted ethical principles that can serve as foundations for a future new culture. They can be used by individuals tuning to the new ethical matrix.

We now find ourselves at the outermost chapters of the Apocalypse: to the left, Chapters 2 through 3—where we will search for signs of the new ethical principles, and to the right, Chapters 21 and 22—on how to embody these principles. Since Part 2 of the present book is dedicated to the basic ethical principles, and how to live and support the process of manifesting Gaia Culture, the study of Chapters 2-3 and Chapters 21-22 can act as a check, as well as perhaps to add some clarity to the values we have already discussed.

In the Apocalypse, the foundations of the new ethics are hidden within Seven Letters sent to the seven early Christian communities in Asia Minor: Ephesus, Smyrna, Pergamon, Thyatira, Sardis, Philadel-phia and Laodicea. The Letters seem to talk about the daily challenges that shook the early Christian communities. But in each Letter I found a key word or sentence that secretly refers to one of the new ethical principles, and the reason it should be practiced. I believe they were hidden because they would compete with the Ten Commandments of Moses, adopted by the Christian church as her own.

The first Letter sent to Ephesus directs our attention to the primeval quality of love. My interpretation of its key message is: 'Follow the voice of the heart'. In each situation, no matter how difficult, be sure to embody the quality and the power of primeval love. The expression 'primeval love' can be understood as love that transcends the loving relationship between human beings. It acts as an all-connecting power of the universal whole and its beings. This can be understood from divine words that show what can be personally achieved by embodying primeval love: 'To the victorious I will give the right to eat from the Tree of Life which grows in the paradise...' (Rev. 2:7) We will get to know the Tree of Life in Chapter 22 as the central axis around which the renewed Earth evolves.

The second Letter sent to Smyrna has the impetus: Do not let a moment of fear throw you off your path of personal or collective destiny. Preserve the inner peace, no matter any given circumstance. We should have faith in advance that in any dramatic situation, success of epochal changes is guaranteed. There is no need to nurture any fear. A massive explosion of fear among humankind could threaten the victorious outcome of the changes that we face in the present epoch.

And what can one expect if one remains steady in upholding his or her inner peace? 'The victorious cannot suffer the slightest hurt from the second death.' (Rev. 2:11) In the language of the Apocalypse, 'the first death' is the natural transition from the embodied reality to the world of ancestors and descendants. 'The second death' would then be that of a given person being erased from the Book of Life, i.e. ceasing to exist as an individual soul.

The third Letter sent to Pergamon highlights the need for changing oneself. Be aware that we have found ourselves in the midst of a universal process of change. Be ready to follow the constant stream of changes. Be attentive not to ignore if some of the many aspects of yourself, or of your activity, are called to change.

And what does the Letter offer as reward for being willing to ceaselessly change? 'I will give the victorious... a white stone with a new name written on it which no man knows except the man who receives it.' (Rev. 2:17) The promise can be understood as obtaining a more advanced level of identity, vibrating beyond the personal self, comprising the whole spectrum of individual identity from the spiritual through the embodied level.

The fourth Letter was sent to Thyatira with the impetus: Be truthful! Check that in any given moment you do not hide some aspect of truth from yourself or from others. Listen again and again to the sound of your heart and examine your mental paths and emotional streams in order to avoid becoming a victim of self-delusion.

Christ's words quoted in the Apocalypse: 'I am the one who searches man's hearts and minds...' (Rev. 2:23)

'To the victorious... I will give the morning star.' (Rev 2:28).

The goal of the spirit of Thyatira is to lead each individual beyond illusion and towards her or his persistence of truth. The morning star is another name for Venus, the star of the Goddess. In a hidden way, the quality of being truthful is associated with the spark of feminine divinity: the Goddess within each human being, regardless of gender.

The fifth Letter, sent to Sardis, prompts us to remain aware of our 'whole', composed of many layers and different dimensions—not just the cosmic levels, held high by spiritual movements. But just as important are the levels in the 'lower' (deeper) grounding vibrations—earthly, elemental, or sub-elemental levels. Told in the words of the Apocalypse: 'I know that you have a reputation for being alive, but that in fact you are dead.' (Rev. 3:2) The words 'alive' and 'dead' in this verse are not referring to mortality, but are synonyms for light and dark, meant to affirm the necessity to integrate both manifested and causal dimensions of existence if we want to be whole.

The reward for balancing relationships with all aspects of life is formulated like this: 'The victorious shall wear white garments, and never shall I erase his name from the Book of Life.' (Rev. 3:5)

The sixth Letter was sent to Philadelphia with the impetus: Be true to yourself! Do not forget who you are and to which ideals you have given a *Wow* to for this incarnation. Remember your spiritual purpose again and again.

The corresponding key word of Revelation does not clarify much: 'You have been faithful to my message and have not denied my name.' (Rev. 3:9) More can be understood from the result of the efforts to be true to oneself: 'As for the victorious, I will make him a pillar in the temple of my God.'

My intuition tells me that behind these words is an attempt to bring awareness that we do not incarnate upon the Earth only for individual development and personal satisfaction. We incarnate on Earth also to offer our individual and group creative action to further the revelation and blossoming of the new Earth and of the transformed universe.

The seventh Letter of Apocalypse is directed to Laodicea to make us aware that we are moving through an age of inevitable decisions.

Each of the oft-questionable situations that we experience, one after another, offers different possibilities. Decide for this or that.

The only thing that one should not afflict upon oneself, in this epoch of grand changes, is to be indecisive. As said in the words of the divine source that sent the Letter: 'I know… that you are neither cold nor hot. I could wish that you were either cold or hot! But since you are lukewarm and neither hot or cold, I intend to spit you out of my mouth!' (Rev. 3:15-16)

These bitter words are an expression of the urgent need to stand firm by decisions that are in tune with the intuition of one's heart. If your decision should prove wrong, be sure that life will offer you another—and if needed, yet another—chance to decide properly.

In its peculiar language, adopted to the spirit of its time, the Apocalypse promises that after learning to decide, while in tune with our inner voice, human beings will be invited to enter our future role that awaits us: 'As for the victorious, I will give him [her] the honour of sitting beside me on my throne, just as I myself won the victory and have taken my seat beside my Father on his throne.' (Rev. 3:21) Obviously the future role of humankind will involve cosmic challenges, beyond our present tasks, inside the Earthly cluster of worlds.

The Earthly cosmos renewed

For a glimpse of how the Earthly universe can change if human beings adopt the code of the new ethics, we need to move forward to Chapters 21 and 22, complements to the 2nd and 3rd chapters. In these two concluding chapters of Revelation, the vision of the New Jerusalem as a matrix of the new space of reality, within which Gaia Culture evolves, is described.

Saint John reports: 'Then one of the seven angels who holds the seven bowls which were filled with the seven last plagues [that in the symmetrical composition of Revelation correspond to the Seven trumpets that blazed after the Seventh seal was broken] came to me and said: Come and I will show you the bride, the wife of the Lamb.' (Rev. 21:9-10)

This is a very remarkable invitation! Since we previously identified the Lamb as Pan, transformed in the spirit of the new constitution of the universe (in the language of the Apocalypse transformed by Christ)… so the wife of the Lamb with seven horns and seven eyes can only be Gaia. She is not the ancient Goddess any more, because she has also gone through the Christ initiation, otherwise she could not start and work with us on developing the new culture.

'Then he carried me away in spirit to the top of a vast mountain, and pointed out to me the city, the holy Jerusalem descending from God out of Heaven… Her brilliance sparkled like a very precious jewel with the clear light of crystal.' (Rev. 21:10-12)

The following portion of the text clarifies that 'New Jerusalem' is not meant as the future Earth, but rather as the matrix or model towards which the process of change is heading. To present it as a model, it has to be created precisely inside the corresponding archetype: 'The one who was talking to me had a golden rod in his hand with which to measure the city, its gateways and its walls. The city lies foursquare, its length equal to its breadth.' (Rev. 21:15-16)

Looking at the matrix of the new Earth's constitution, we are shown that the matter composing the new manifested Earth is of a different kind of matter than is known today. Matter is becoming translucent so that subtle dimensions of reality, that can not presently express through matter, will appear in the embodied world in their own way. To point to the different quality of matter, the Apocalypse uses the symbol of 12 precious stones and gold: 'The wall itself was built of a translucent stone, while the city was of purest gold, with the brilliance of glass. The foundation stones of the wall of the city were fashioned out of every kind of precious stones. The first foundation-stone was Jasper, the second sapphire, the third chalcedony…' (Rev. 21:18-20)

The second quality of the new Earth is the astonishing absence of any sanctuaries. It is because the new Earth, its cultures, and the life flourishing there, are sacred in themselves. Said in the language of Revelation: 'I could see no Sanctuary in the city, for the Lord, the Almighty God and the Lamb are themselves its sanctuary.' (Rev. 21:22-23)

The third quality, of interest to our research, says that the light illuminating the New Earth will not come from outside but from within the planet, and from the inside of the universal whole: 'The city has no need for the light of the Sun or Moon, for the splendour of God fills it with light and its radiance is the lamb.' (Rev. 21:24)

The fourth quality is very briefly presented with the symbol of the city's gates, open day and night. The permanently open gates can be identified with the interdimensional portals through which inhabitants of the future Gaia Culture can communicate with the parallel worlds.

The fifth quality of the New Jerusalem is its economy, based on the permanent flow of life energy through the streets of the city. The symbolic language that must always enclose the name of God to avoid the notion of blasphemy says it like this: 'Then he showed me the river of the Water of life, sparkling like crystal as it flowed from the throne of God and of the Lamb.' (Rev. 22:1-2)

The sixth quality inherent in the matrix of the New Earth is expressed through the symbol of the Tree of Life. It is an important symbol because it contrasts with '[Eden's] Tree of Distinction [between good and bad]', and characterizes the ending of our present evolution. In the language of the Jewish Bible, it is marked by the act of expelling Adam and Eve from Paradise. This act represents entering the difficult era of our history, where we are permanently confronted with challenges bringing good or bad experiences, so as to learn to distinguish what is beneficial and what is destructive to life.

The Tree of Life, on the contrary, is a symbol for that which makes the streams of life flow in an intertwining way, connecting various levels of existence in a cyclic manner. Under the shadow of the Tree of Life—speaking symbolically—we will develop our human selves, by meeting countless creative challenges and opportunities, instead of constantly falling into difficulty. The Apocalypse touches upon this important sequence of change in a very condensed form: '... and on either bank of the river grew the Tree of Life...' (Rev. 22:2) Interestingly this statement is contrary to logic. How can a tree grow on both sides of a river? I interpret this statement as a sign that the Tree of Life stands for the principle that transcends any dualism, like the above-mentioned dualism of bad and good.

The seventh, and last, quality of the New Jerusalem, very briefly marks: 'The leaves of the Tree [of Life] were for the healing of the nations.' (Rev. 22:2) This short sentence feels hopeful for the future home of humanity, thus opening the door to the following chapters of our Gaia Culture book, dealing with the relationships in human society.

Gaia Culture without Gaia

After I wrote the last sentence above I retired to bed. That night, 4 to 5 January 2021, I had a dream that commanded me to rethink the whole section about the Revelation of Saint John:

In my dream I am shown a large building in the form of a square. Even though the building is of a modern type, I am astonished that it has the same form as the model of the New Jerusalem. When I enter the building, together with my wife, I am overwhelmed by its perfect inner organization. There I find everything that human culture needs like a huge conference hall, theatre, cinema… but I do not find anything there to drink or to eat.

I walk with my wife outside the building into a large park that surrounds it. I am taken with its spaciousness, but notice that all trees have an identical form. This is unnatural and strange to me. We meet a foreign man in the park who obviously knows the history of the building and its surroundings. He lets us know that originally the place was a stony and deserted landscape. Praising human achievement, he expresses regret that after the construction of the magnificent building, some minor buildings were added to cover the need of a kitchen and some storage.

Pondering the message of my dream of the New Jerusalem, I became aware that indeed no nature or anything natural appeared in this matrix of the new planetary space. How could the trees in my dream have been of identical form? There is not one appearance in nature that can be identical to another. Even each snowflake is formed differently from all other billions of snowflakes.

But, what really made me rethink the foundations of the Apocalypse was the story the foreign man told, asserting that the building was positioned on barren ground. This also explained the lack of nature and the unnatural stand of trees. Nature would not thrive on barren ground. It reminded me of the words of the angel, cited above, whilst he showed the New Jerusalem to Saint John, as being brought from Heaven down to the Earth.

Here, I must state clearly that we are primarily interested in the New Jerusalem that grows *from* the Earth, whose growth is also tuned to the universal matrix, projected down nearly two millennia ago. Its descent was perceived and formulated in the words of the Revelation of Saint John. Maybe we should not demand from the Apocalypse more than that. To support Gaia Culture's growth from the ground up—not from the barren, but from the fertile ground of the Earth—is the task of our generation and of future generations.

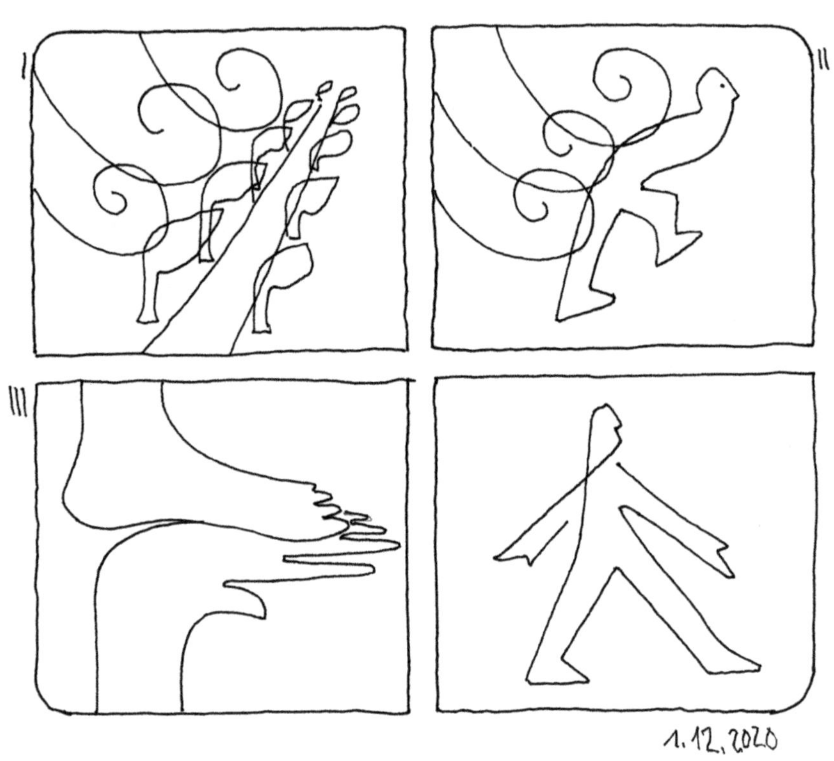

I
II
III
1. 12. 2020

EXERCISES 3

With Gaia messages

01.12.2020

Human beings—honour your connectedness
to your body.
Hold it steady,
even if 'time and time again' events, incidents,
and situations in the outer world
disturb your connection with your body.
Perceive it, become conscious of it
and then, reconnect.
My support is all yours.
If only you will allow this new experience,
you will recognize it.
Faithfully I stand by your side—
in difficult times.
We accompany each other in difficult times,
become increasingly aware of this.
(Gaia)

- You are walking along a long straight path, lined with trees and hedges.
- A terrible wind is blowing, threatening to sweep you away from your path.
- Imagine that with each step, you place your foot not only on the ground, but also on Gaia's open hand.
- With every step you take, feel how the touch of Gaia's hand firmly roots you in the earth element, so that you cannot be swept away from your path, no matter what you encounter in life.
- Gaia's loving touch gives you support and inspires you to follow your inner path.

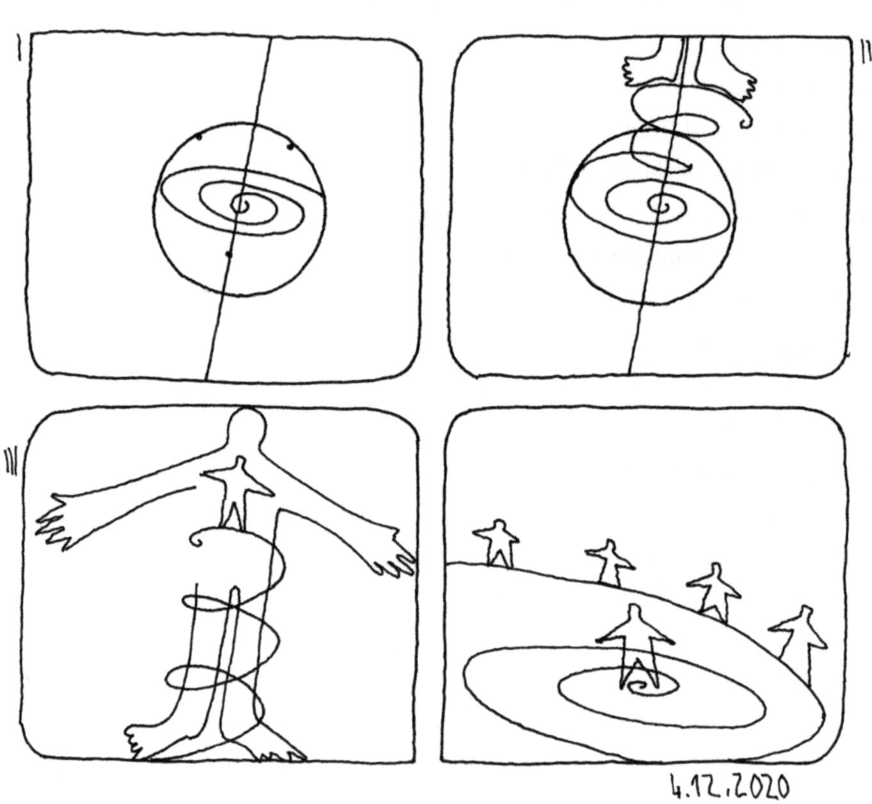

4.12.2020

04.12.2020

Human beings—we are uniting.
Your activated heart energy grows more present.
Gaia receives it—your heart energy—
and amplifies it through her presence,
which you humans are becoming even more aware of.
Stand united.
Together keep your creatorship alive.
(Michael)

- Imagine that a fine golden spiral begins to develop in the centre of the Earth. It expands horizontally until the spiral has the width of the equator.
- It then begins to rise in the direction of your body—still spiralling. It contracts progressively, until it is so narrow that it can just touch the soles of your feet.
- The golden spiral then lifts you higher and higher, up to the level of your heart.
- Here you can take a break and listen to the dialogue between the Earth's heart and your heart.
- Afterwards, the golden spiral brings you back to the ground. It spreads out so far that it can reach people close to you. The expansion continues until all those people are touched who are ready to vibrate in harmony with Earth's heart.

7.12.2020

07.12.2020

Human beings—if you turn the eye of your heart
more frequently towards me,
I awaken deeper into my own presence.
Your heart's perspective, free and courageous,
enables my journey towards healing.
Simultaneously the chance for healing opens up to you.
Together we discover
the potential of this path.
It is in your freedom
to walk this path.
(Gaia)

- Become aware that the Earth is not under your feet, but breathing all around you, for it is, above all, a cosmic consciousness.
- Take the time to sense this image deep within you.
- Experience your heart space as a centre point around which Gaia has expanded her creation.
- Then invite Gaia to enter this centre and, from your heart space, animate her creation.
- Let your inner gaze wander around the space that surrounds you, to see what the rest of the world feels like when Gaia is present in your heart centre.
- She may stay there, for the heart space is wide enough for both of you.

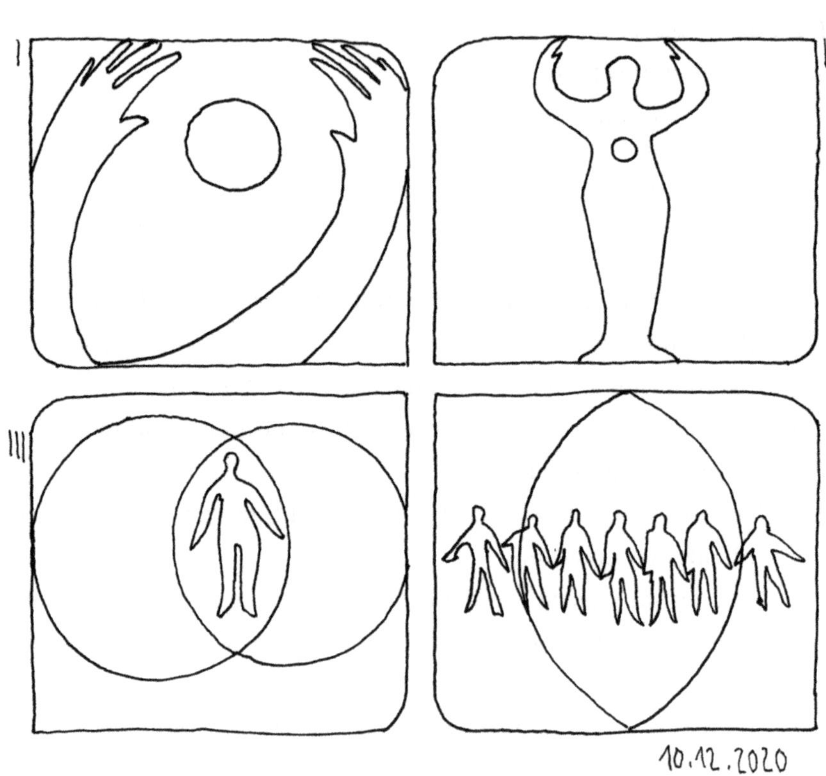
10.12.2020

10.12.2020

- The Earth is a temple dedicated to the essence of life.
- Imagine a pillar of light rising from its centre with a golden sphere floating in the middle of it.
- Now perceive that your body is also a temple surrounded by a column of light, with a golden sphere floating in the centre of your heart.
- The moment the two spheres perceive each other, they unite and the column in the temple becomes so wide that you too are standing in it.
- Feel how thoroughly you are grounded by this.
- Visualize consciously how the column becomes wider and wider so that an increasing number of people find room in it.
- The united spheres are radiating so strongly that the hearts of the people within them awaken.

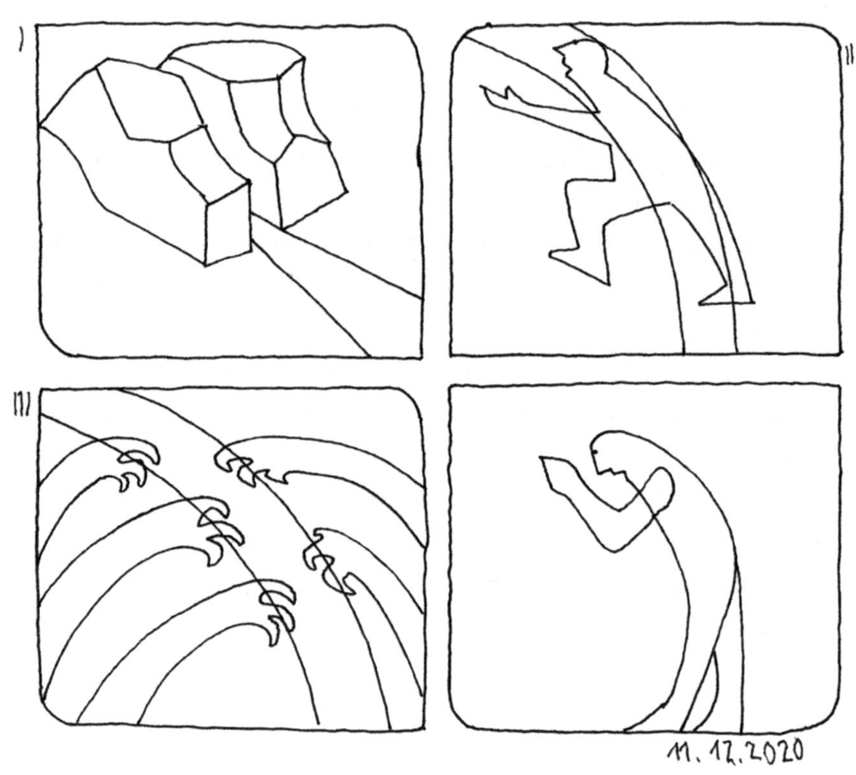

11. 12. 2020

11.12.2020

Human beings—
free yourselves into
your true essence
and thus, experience my true essence.
Look behind the super-imposed veils
of times gone by.
Walk through them—into the new time.
Upheaval everywhere.
Without sacrifices there are
no new opportunities.
Let go.
(Gaia)

- Imagine you are on a path and have reached a very narrow passage between two rocks.
- The passage is long like a gorge and so narrow that you cannot slip through.
- However, you do not let yourself be intimidated and you climb into it.
- As the passage is narrower than your physical body, all foreign layers are stripped from you as you slip through.
- The mineral particles swallow these foreign layers little by little and lock them into their atomic structures, where they will be transformed over millions of years.
- At the end of the narrow passage, thank the beings of the mineral world for offering relief to you. Continue to follow your path and no longer let your presence be tainted with fear, alien thoughts, and self-alienation.

12.12.2020

12.12.2020

Human beings—
see the wealth within you rather than around you.
Go into thyself, descend into thyself, and listen to me.
Contemplate with me your opportunities
in this time of change.
Potentialities of the new—
seize them, experience them, in our connectedness.
(Gaia)

- Imagine that your eyes are not only in the front of your head, but that you are looking forward from the back of your head.
- What do you see in the cavity of your skull? In it is stored the creative knowledge with which the universe was fashioned.
- How does this wealth that we humans bring to Earth feel?
- Gaia and her elemental worlds need this knowledge to be able to further develop the earthly cosmos.
- The new world, infused with peace and freedom, can be built tomorrow if the knowledge we humans carry within us is coupled with the wisdom of Gaia.

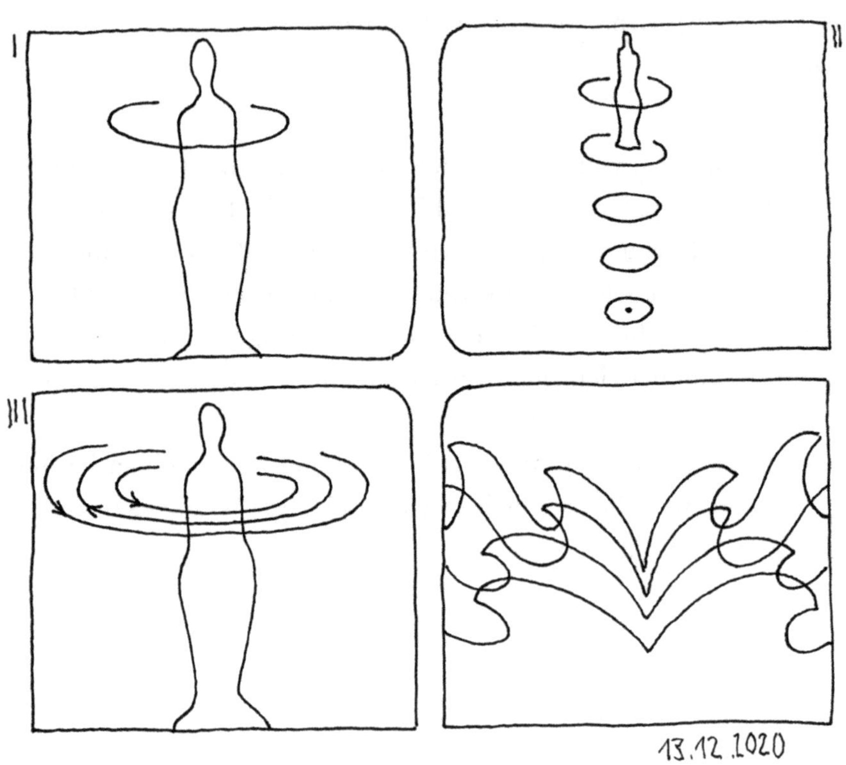
I
II
III
13.12.2020

13.12.2020

Human beings—
acknowledge our interconnectedness.
Everywhere,
with all your senses.
Experience and live
our oneness
the while.
Particularly in this time,
time of omnipresent transformation.
(Gaia)

- Imagine a blue ring solemnly spinning around your body at heart level.
- Let the ring slide into the depths of the Earth, so far that it rotates for a while around the focal point of Gaia, in the centre of the Earth. Listen to the quality that builds up inside you.
- Then bring the ring back up to your heart level.
- Now imagine a second blue ring spinning around this ring, but in the opposite direction.
- Around the second ring revolves a third ring, again in the opposite direction.
- The three counter-revolving rings are sending ripples of strong ring-shaped waves into the force field of humanity, inviting all fellow human beings to connect permanently with Gaia, the Creator of Earth.

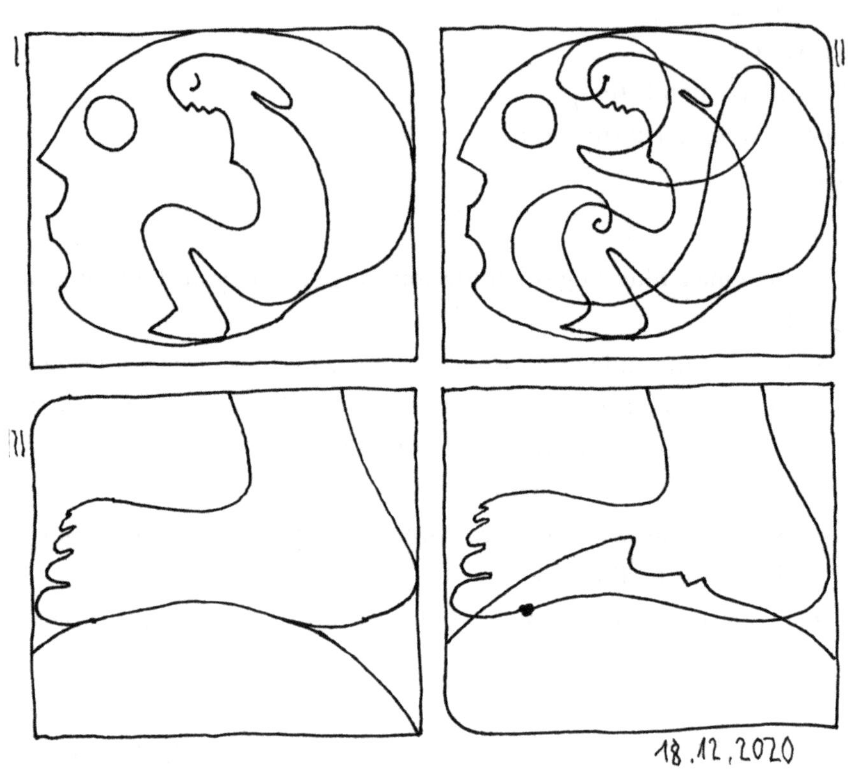

18.12.2020

18.12.2020

Come on, human being—
cast off the shadowy parts of your Self,
abandon your masquerade,
here,
with me.
Reveal yourself to me—
authentic and true,
otherwise we will lose each other—
lose the vitality of our Oneness.
(Gaia)

- Imagine that you are sitting inside your skull.
- Not that you are that small, but that the sphere of your head is large enough to accommodate you in a sitting position.
- Sense the feeling of the sphere of your consciousness completely penetrating and surrounding you.
- Then turn your attention to the soles of your feet that are touching both the periphery of your head's sphere and also Earth's sphere in this position.
- Feel the soles of your feet as mediators of the close and loving relationship between your consciousness and the presence of Gaia.

PART 4: RECREATING HUMAN SOCIETY

Threefold communication

It is now time to discuss practical communication with the parallel worlds. We need to come to the realization that we are not alone on the planet. We share its multidimensional space with other intelligent beings that are very much interested in how future human society will be composed. The formation of this new society should not be limited to human beings, but should also tune to those worlds that are closest to us, such as the world of elemental beings at the side of Gaia and the sphere of human ancestors and descendants at the side of the spiritual worlds. I will try to lead a conversation between chosen representatives from these two worlds, with me as a representative of embodied human beings.

Of course we will not meet in a conference hall, neither can we talk to each other in a bar, nor over a social media platform of the Internet.

I will make the effort to tune to the voiceless proposals of both my partners, translating their contributions into logical language. But before starting our conversation on different aspects of the new emerging human society, I need first to present my two partners in the dialogue.

I have earlier mentioned a master of the elemental world called Julius; if you remember, he taught me how to enter the Apocalypse through the right door. I know him from the stony island in the Adriatic Sea where I used to go on a yearly retreat to work on preparing future book projects. Julius helped me first to establish links with the elemental world while I was preparing the book, *Elemental Beings and Nature Spirits*. Later we collaborated excellently while I was working on decoding the 'Fifth Gospel' of Jesus the Christ, published later as *Christ Power and Earth Wisdom*. It was on that occasion that I realized that masters of the elemental world have access to the complete memory of the Earth, including human history to its finest detail. This easily qualified Julius to represent Gaia in our talk about recreating human society.

From my dear deceased friends from the spiritual sphere, I invited Ruth to take part in our conversation. She joined my geomantic and Earth healing work in the early nineties of the last century and has since not missed any of my workshops held in the German language. Her background was in anthroposophy, founded by the Austrian spiritual teacher and artist Rudolf Steiner. As a retired teacher in the Waldorf school system, Ruth was invited to join a small community in Bavaria that began to work with Rudolf Steiner several decades after his death. They helped him to continue his research by developing new remedies, according to his instructions. A clairvoyant woman who took part in the group telepathically received his messages. When Ruth approached my work, the community and research centre no longer existed because the key members had already died. She joined them in the spiritual world in the year 2005, when she died during our bus travel to Asia Minor, where I held a line of workshops at the archeological remains of the seven ancient cities that we know from the Apocalypse's chapter on the seven Letters sent to the seven early Christian communities in Asia Minor.

In presenting my partners, I must also make clear that they may have different positions than myself, being that I am incarnated in a human body. Julius, as a representative of the elemental world, for example, is not exactly an individual being as we humans are. When he talks, he speaks as an expression of the totality of the elemental world, Gaia, its creator included—even if he has his own individual connection to me as my partner in dialogue. But the knowledge that he transmits should be understood as a compilation of Gaia's wisdom and memory.

Similarly the individual souls inhabiting the world of ancestors and descendants should not be perceived in too much of a personalized way. If a soul that has gone through all stages of the after-death process speaks, its words reflect—besides its individual tones—the noosphere (consciousness sphere) of the spiritual world as a vast whole, including human ancestors and descendants and the spiritual teachers, often called ascended masters.

In describing my conversations with the elemental world and dear friends from the spiritual sphere, I must emphasize that I do not perceive my partners as being far away. On the contrary, I feel them—while communicating only—present within myself. To say more exactly, I experience the resonance of their presence within my body. Yet each of their resonance is focused in a clearly different location. I feel the resonance of Julius focused around the lower end of my breastbone at the seat of the, before-mentioned, Personal Elemental. As a member of the spiritual world, I perceive Ruth in the larger space of my head, including the throat area.

Community

For our first meeting I invited Julius and Ruth to the former monastery of Santa Elena, positioned in the very southern tip of the urban composition of Venice. According to my insight of ancient times, representatives of the three worlds (elemental, spiritual and human), that we three are today representing, regularly met at this former island in the Venetian lagoon.

Julius, the master of the elemental world, was the first to answer my invitation. He resembles an ancient Greek philosopher. Ruth arrived in her light body surrounded by a bright aura.

I started the conversation on the future human community with the question: 'Dear Ruth, 15 years have passed since you left behind the community of embodied humans. Looking back, how do you perceive your experience?'

In answer, the space of my head became as narrow as the throat. In effect, she showed me the human community as closed in a vertical cylinder. The moment of death could be described as the soul pulling itself out from this cylinder and expanding in the free space of the spiritual world. I understood the conditions to breathe and create in human society to be extremely narrow.

The commentary of Julius, relating to the same question, was different. He let a solid wall rise vertically through my body, dividing it into two halves. Julius, as a representative of the elemental world of Gaia, pulled himself backward to be hidden behind the wall. The space in front of the wall, identified with human society, I felt as empty. I felt the environment, in which we as society exist, as impoverished by the pushing of the living presence of the elemental world into the (invisible) back-space of the manifested world.

It is clear that to build a new human society both of these general blockades, restricting the freedom and connectedness of present-day human society, need to be abolished. But what can be done practically to create a more free space for human society?

Without hesitation Julius answered the question by pointing to the origin of dragon powers within the human being, located at the bottom of the belly. His answer was a surprise to me because I expected our intellect to be the problem, in that it refuses even the idea that nature knows its own spiritual (causal) dimensions. But then I realized that Julius actually pointed to a dark spot occupying my coccyx area. Based on my Earth healing work in different landscapes with suppressed primeval powers of life—the so called dragon lines—I understood Julius. If the natural flow of dragon powers in our human body is blocked and suppressed at the coccyx area, then there is an essential lack of the energy needed to build peaceful and co-creative human society.

But Ruth wanted to formulate it in a different way. She directed my memory to the first Letter of the Apocalypse, sent to the community of Ephesus, which speaks to the connection we are discussing; a specific dragon power is missing—called 'primeval love'. If the gate at the coccyx is closed, then the required flow of dragon power is prevented from reaching the human heart area to be transformed into love power. It is the primeval love power that is capable of nourishing human loving and constructive openness towards other human beings, the basis of a grounded and peaceful human community.

Julius, representing the elemental world, proposed the following imagination to transcend the blockade:

- The world we live in is a multi-storey house, with rooms one above another.

- Sit in meditation on the second floor, being present in your heart space.
- At the same time, sit in meditation three storeys lower in the deep cellar of the house. The cellar is, in effect, a cave with walls covered with wonderful crystals where the dragons of Gaia frequent.
- Be aware of aligning yourself perfectly with the second self, sitting in the cellar, so that you are in resonance with each other.
- Now become aware that a third aspect of you is sitting in meditation three storeys higher on the fifth floor, representing the spiritual world. Align yourself also with this part of you.
- Now bring your attention to the flow between the three levels and feel its quality. Repeat the exercise as often as possible.

My concluding words are that it is not realistic to expect that the whole of humanity will at once be enthusiastic about creating societies based upon the principle of primeval love flowing among its participants. My proposal is to create smaller communities as islands in the middle of the more and more chaotic cyber-tech society. There is no need to live together at common places. The connecting bonds can be created and sustained in a telepathic way—love at a distance that doesn't know distance.

Society inspired by the plants

To discuss the composition of our future society, I invited my dialogue partners again to Venice, this time to the Island of Cypresses. This island is positioned on the other side of the large watery surface of Bacino San Marco, in front of the Ducal palace. It is better known as the island of San Giorgio Maggiore, named after the famous basilica of the same name, built in the Renaissance style by Andrea Palladio.

I chose this place in response to an insight of a few years ago about the original role of the place before it was Christianized in the early Middle Ages through the building of a monastery, dedicated to the dragon-killer Saint George. Originally the island was (and secretly still is) the seat of advanced elemental beings, the so-called 'Devas', that treasure and radiate the archetypal patterns for the use of the plant world in organizing itself. Why is the plant world important to the future organization of human society?

Not long ago I had a peculiar dream in which I was shown human homes positioned at the tops of trees. In the dream, that has an important place in my book *Dancing with the Earth Changes*, I saw people communicating among themselves with the help of plants they hold in their hands. This was the reason I wanted to meet at San Giorgio Island to talk about the theme of human society.

Julius, the master of the elemental world, proposed searching for the key in the chapters of the Seven Seals in the Apocalypse (discussed in the last section of this book). The first seal tells of the Earth's cosmic transition from Element-Earth to an era ruled by the Element-Air. Air replaces the Earth-Element's rather static and dry matter with a lighter and freely movable quality of consciousness as a base for future evolution.

Further, Julius points out a parallel transition of humankind brought about by the exchanging of the ruling Element. To establish our evolution by Gaia, for millions of years we were guided by the animal archetypes to develop our bodies, including our organs, abilities of perception, of thought, and emotion. It has been beautiful sharing our bodily and emotional experiences with the animal kingdom. Their sacrifice made it possible for us to survive in and to enjoy the beauty and splendours of the materialized world. But this gift included the innate shadows of the animal kingdom. Survival instincts necessary for animals, and for our past, such as the never-ending battle for resources, territories, and ruling positions, have no place in future human culture. Now is the time to move to another track governed by plant archetypes.

Plants are beings of silence. They express themselves through the art and form of their presence, following the natural cycles of transformations. What we as human beings should learn from plants is the way they hold perfect order in their world without ruling hierarchies, bureaucracies, plans, or restrictions. They are connected among themselves through telepathic networks and collaborate perfectly with elemental beings on one side and microorganisms, viruses and fungi on the other. The Gaia Culture society should develop a similar inner organization that allows more space for inner growth and creative freedom to all its members.

At this point I became aware that the counter-forces, in an attempt to prevent a shift to this 'Vegan' evolutionary track, have created a similar, but fake, condition in modern human society. Plant intercommunication methods are being copied, in the developing of cybernetics, as a technical means of connecting us on a planetary scale—but a connection without a heart-to-heart or even bodily presence. The inherently impersonal communication of technology allows a relatively small group of people, a so-called 'Deep State', to divide and control all levels of social organization, keeping us in constant turmoil and conflict.

Ruth, representing the spiritual world, entered the conversation by stressing that the plant world is organized along three horizontal (nonhierarchical) levels, not just the two already mentioned (the telepathic network of plant organism and collaboration with elemental beings, fungi, viruses and microorganisms). The third level, as already mentioned above, is guidance by the 'Devas'. Devas are highly evolved elemental beings that treasure and radiate the matrix for each plant species and also for different biotopes. Since plants and elemental beings are always connected to the 'sound' of their corresponding Deva-consciousness, there is never a moment of confusion concerning their long-term development.

In the case of human society, this third level also exists. It is highly respected by the aboriginal cultures, but ignored by modern societies: the autonomous world of our ancestors and descendants, or the 'spiritual world'. There exist groups of souls, advanced in their evolution, who create possible patterns of development for each soul incarnated upon Earth, for each nation and race. Ruth points out that if we, walking upon the Earth, were to listen inwardly to their inspiration, we could perceive advice on how to lead our lives and take part in our societies, without removing our freedom of choice. We are free to choose among different possibilities offered. The important advantage is that patterns of inspiration, arriving from the sources of the spiritual world, are in tune with the matrix of being human and the general matrix of the cosmic evolution. This would be an enormous help navigating among the innumerable possibilities offered by the manifested world.

If I am allowed a final word, then it is to stress that the future Gaia Culture is not meant to copy the plant kingdom. We are different, but a much younger evolution upon the Earth than plants. The time is ripe to choose them, our more experienced teachers, as close companions on our path through the challenges of the embodied world sphere.

Education as initiation

My third session with my three-petal group took place at Santa Marta. Santa Marta is positioned at the opposite side of Venice from our first meeting place of Santa Elena. It once stood on a narrow peninsula, three sides surrounded by waters of the lagoon. (The Gothic building of Santa Marta is an architectural martyr. When this part of Venice was degraded to a commercial port, the church was similarly degraded for use as a storehouse. Only after the port recently lost its function was Santa Marta restored as a cultural hall.) It stands on the site that in ancient times served as a ritual meeting place between dolphins and elemental beings of Water.

Working with groups in the field of geomancy and Earth healing, I have discovered that there is a way to hand the leadership of certain parts of human education over to the beings of nature and the landscape, foremost to the stones, trees, and rivers. As part of the Gaia consciousness, they are capable of teaching through experience. If individuals tune to their presence, then beings of nature can inspire with new insights and valuable knowledge that cannot be transmitted via usual methods of education. I am very interested in the opinions of my two partners about this approach to education.

Ruth took to the message. She confirmed that learning from Gaia and her spheres is equally important for the souls that are between two incarnations, even as they abide in the spiritual sphere. They travel along the 'paths of the soul'—kind of ley lines—visiting sacred places on Earth; places known and, as yet, unknown to us. Each of these places has certain interdimensional portals through which they can be approached. The Earth, as Gaia, is a proper Book of Life, with knowledge written in the form of sacred places positioned on its surface, in the underground, and in its atmosphere. Each of them transmits different knowledge via experience. Innumerable paths for souls have been created since the distant past so that all these places can be approached, together composing a gigantic university.

Julius, the master of the elemental world of course, was enthusiastic about my idea of collaborative learning, the back and forth flow between beings of nature and human groups and individuals. He stressed that beings of nature and the elemental world also want to grow spiritually and are eager to learn from human beings those qualities and aspects of knowledge that are the heritage of human evolution. In past ages people lived close to animals and plants, also using stones to create their tools. Since then, the awful distance that has grown between us can only be bridged through conscious effort; with exercises of attunement to each other or by redeveloping our sensibility with the help of exercises dedicated to widened perception.

He added that he understood that humans also need to develop those abilities that are more or less exclusively ours; such as, the logical ways of thinking, the mastery of decision, the living laws of ethics, mastery in arts and sciences etc. But if the education in these fields is detached from Gaia's Book of Life, then we will have missed the reason as to why our cosmic evolution directed us to incarnate upon the Earth.

Water-based communication

Modern communication has become more and more dependent on cybernetics, in other words, dependent on electricity and the Element-Fire. It is much more convenient giving a lecture to a group of people on a computer screen, eliminating thousands of miles of travel. It is also ecologically just. But the question I wished to ask is how much does the fiery nature of cyber-language distort communication, making it dry, inciting conflict, and potentially allowing it to be manipulated? In effect, I wished to talk to my partners about the possible alternatives of communication, in tune with the visions and needs of evolving Gaia Culture.

In answer to the question, Ruth stressed that communication should be a means of creating communion between people, also between humankind and parallel world spheres. It should not be taken just as casual talk, but as a constant flow of living relationships, a network permanently connecting beings and worlds. It is this basic flow of communication that, at moments when it is needed, transforms dialogue into words of connection among partners—and afterwards descends back into the network of silent heart-to-heart communicative flow.

Julius added that if we do not want communication paths to burn out, creating conflicting situations, there must be a transference of the involved Elements. Fire, as the base element of cybernetic communication, needs to be exchanged with the element of Water. Human society must also be taught the incredible capacities of water for storing information. 'You, as humans, must be asking how this idea could be put into practice. Of course you do not know what to us, as elemental beings, is natural. Water existing at the subtle levels, usually called "astral", can be translated as "liquid of the stars" (in Latin *astrum* means "the star")'.

I had to apologize for interrupting Julius at this point, but I needed to explain my experiences of telepathic workshops and to ask the elemental master if his idea was on this same path. After March 2020, due to the so-called 'Covid pandemic', travel was discontinued. I had the inspiration to create telepathic workshops, working together, with interested people, located on different parts of the globe. Each time I would start by preparing a plan with exercises to be done in an imaginative form, which I would e-mail to participants. Also, instead of the group starting the programme simultaneously, time would relate to the course of the Sun. For example, everyone would start at 9:00 in the morning following the rising Sun, regardless of in which part of the globe she or he lived.

Through the sharing of our experiences after the workshop, we found that participants would often have deep and meaningful insights and intuitions. Working together over large distances gave the feeling we were moving together in the landscape, similar to when we would work in natural environments. Working in the telepathic way felt like creating in another Element, one that was neither Air, nor Fire, and certainly not Earth. My question to Julius: Was this the method of communication that he was suggesting?

His response was that we are moving into the age of synergies, so we should not limit ourselves to the use of one Element. A network of the magnetic Water-Element—as carrier of information—should be complemented with the Fire of inspiration, fuelling the movement of that information. The resulting combination of impulses carried by water is, of course, useless if there are no beings with consciousness—represented by the Air-Element—capable of catching the message and translating it into words or ideas.

My remark to Julius was that he had addressed the elements of Water, Fire, and Air in cooperation; but have we lost the element Earth?

Ruth asked: Are you not an artist? Is art not a means of communication that can combine all four Elements including the Earth? I cannot imagine a work of art that is not embodied in stone, in colour, in movement, or in words...

I happily agreed! For decades I have searched for a new art form that would function, not only as a separate human creation, but also with a basic role in everyday life. I can imagine art that would, in the framework of Gaia Culture, enable us to express high levels of communication; for example, rituals performed among members of human families or the exchanging of ideas or messages with beings from other world spheres. In this case, we might dance a message, or paint one, perhaps sculpt it in stone; not as an exhibition or theatre piece, but as the optimal method for the communication of especially complex messages.

Individual vs. collective

Modern civilization exhibits extreme divisions between individuals, tending toward the egocentric (inhabiting the Western world) and more collectivistic societies (mostly from the East), like old Soviet Russia or present-day China. Is the existence of a more balanced society possible, where excessive individualism does not need to be balanced by autocratic rulers that control by suppressing freedom?

As usual the elemental master was the first to enter the dialogue. He stressed that a collective consciousness is something normal, and appreciated in his world sphere. Being part of what he calls 'group consciousness' is not oppressive, as humans might believe. For elemental beings, it represents a means of staying permanently rooted in the noosphere of Gaia. Even more importantly, it provides the dependability of mutual support. Group consciousness allows life energy or knowledge, accessible to one part of the group, if needed, to be moved immediately to support a momentarily weak member of the group. Collective awareness is not static, but is an ever-balancing movement, benefiting each member of the group, and through this balancing act, the group as a whole.

Ruth added to the words of Julius that the co-creative exchange between the elemental world of Gaia and humankind is a basic necessity for the constitution of Gaia Culture. Elemental beings can teach us how we as humans can relate to each other by creating our own kind of group awareness, while we can teach elemental beings how to become more self-aware and autonomous in their contribution to Gaia's creation.

To clarify his message, Julius proposed the following exercise:

- Go to a forest and breathe deeply for a while.
- Now imagine that along with the air, you are inhaling the trees. Imagine them as just a part of the mass of minute microorganisms that we always inhale with our breathing.
- During the exhale let the trees return to their places. Continue to breathe this way for a while.

- Take some time to feel the joyous and dancing communion of the forest. If you do not feel it, repeat the exercise or go and embrace a tree.

This discussion with my partners helped me to realize one of the reasons why the modern model of democracy has failed. It is not possible to form happy and creative human societies if our democracy stays closed in the bubble of human affairs and relationships. Future democracy must be a 'Pan-Democracy'—'Pan' standing in ancient Greek for an all-connecting quality. We need to find ways to extend our democratic ideas and institutions to include the spheres of other evolutions with which we share the planet Earth as a common home; first of all, the planetary community of the elemental beings.

New approach to religion

The Latin base for 'religion' (*re-ligare*) means, 'to reconnect'. Religion can be understood as a basic need of human beings to be connected to Earth and to the Cosmos and to find ways of recreating those links again and again. I started with the question to Julius of how the reconnection issue looks, as seen from the point of view of the elemental world.

Julius: Perceiving human beings as they practice something that you would call 'reconnecting', is a rather painful experience in our world due to two problematic issues. Either you connect in an abstract way to a spiritual ideal, for example to the one you call 'God', that we cannot feel as something existing in the here and now. Or you detach from all spiritual levels and plunge yourself into the whirlpool of superficial life, which from our perception, results in you disappearing from true reality. Often you mix the two, jumping back and forth—say, going to the supermarket then praying in a church. This we find the most annoying. In all these cases we cannot perceive you as present. You float around as shadows. Beware; step-by-step you are losing the right to continue your evolution upon the Earth.

Ruth agreed that indeed there are two paths of reconnection needed to eliminate this poisonous dualistic pattern:

> On one hand, you, as the human race, exist parallel in two world spheres, spiritual and embodied. You need to connect to the common source of existence, which can be called the all-connecting Divinity; otherwise you are divided into two separate spheres. When remaining in the manifested world only, you are too dispersed and your human communities too weak. You need to uphold a common spiritual focus—the all-connecting divinity. Depending on your religious or spiritual background, this, perhaps, might be imagined in different ways.
>
> But connection to divinity as the common and all-connecting focus is meaningless, leading back to the old religious patterns, if you, as individuals, are not present in the given moment and do not move with the constant flow of change. As Julius put it, the connection to the divine source becomes abstract if you, as a human race, are not vibrating simultaneously in a heartfelt connection to the essence of Gaia and her elemental worlds— which, in your case, is achieved only individually. As I mentioned before, even we in the spiritual worlds must go again and again on pilgrimages to the sacred places of the Earth, so as not to lose our grounding in the spiritual realms of Gaia.

If I, Marko, may summarize our discussion of the emerging spirituality related to the Gaia Culture; there are two paths to walk as one. On one hand we need to individually care for our personal integrity, grounding, and connectedness, while at the same time, work on awakening collective sensitivity to Gaia and her elemental worlds. On the other hand, the ever-renewing relationship to the Gaia worlds needs to be intertwined with our common dedication to the all-connecting divine principle—while retaining our own individual attributes, of course.

No less important is that we, being part of different groups and communities working within the same emerging Gaia Culture, make efforts to develop our visions and relevant imaginations of those qualities that we feel as our connecting principles, as next we should create rituals and different kinds of celebrations to express and ground our spiritual aspirations.

Economy of exchange

To open our talk on Gaia Culture economy I would like to briefly present the Integral Green Economy. I am a collaborator in this movement that develops its projects in different countries worldwide—one country of which is my own, Slovenia. The movement is based upon a scheme developed by my friends, Alexander Schieffer and Ronnie Lessem. It refers to an archetype where four building blocks are positioned at four cardinal points of a circle, around a fifth central principle. The four collaborating aspects of economy are:

- science, systems and technology (social knowledge based economy);
- finance and enterprise (life based economy);
- nature and community (self-sufficient community-based economy);
- culture and spirituality (developmental culture based economy).

The fifth aspect, at the centre of the circle, represents a base of activities for the other four and is called the 'moral core'.

I asked Julius to comment on the opinion of the elemental world concerning this scheme.

'It is obvious', says Julius, with the help of feelings that sprout inside my body:

that the Integral Green Economy is developed exclusively within the bubble of the human world. It feels as if the Earth, with the potentials of her elemental consciousness and life force, is ignored. The plan itself is excellent, and it would work well in the future culture, if not for the fact that all our evolutions are at the crossroads of universal transformation at our basic level of existence. Under these conditions, exclusively

> leaning on human potential to nourish humanity and to secure the aspired social justice will not have the required strength. The word 'integral' should also embrace the other worlds of the Earth's cluster so as not to leave humanity alone to struggle with increasingly more violent 'climate changes'.

I feel as though present-day human economy is ignorant of the inexhaustible reservoir of life energy that keeps us, and all other manifested beings, alive. If our economy and connected technologies would accept the communication and free flow of energy between the causal and manifested worlds, then we could eliminate all our exploiting methodologies for generating energy—hydroelectric, fossil fuel combustion, wind power, solar energy etc.

Julius added (with a critical attitude) that even the efforts of our most brilliant scientists in developing 'zero energy' technologies, are in vain. All of these energies function through the forced manipulation of elemental consciousness. Without direct communication and cooperation with the elemental world of Gaia, these technologies are as unsustainable as the burning of fossil fuels. But communicating with the elemental world is not possible without changing our attitude towards Gaia, as creator of the Earthly universe, and developing an intimate heart-to-heart relationship with her and her co-creative beings.

If I understood Julius properly, he accepted the four aspects of the Integral Green Economy, but he would expand the centre of the scheme, called 'the moral core'. Instead of leaning only on human ethical principles—which are, of course, a precondition for a new kind of economy—he would add to the centre of the new economy matrix a living and loving relationship to Gaia and her elemental worlds. The cooperation between humankind and parallel world spheres of Gaia is the precondition for a new kind of economy that does not harm any aspect of life and its beings, enabling the free flow of energy and information between all worlds manifested and those not manifested.

Democracy yes, but how?

Democracy is an ancient Greek invention that was reactivated in modern times. The United States of America was the first to establish the new pattern of democracy. It took almost two hundred years for the European Union (EU) to follow. The main problem with democracy was introduced at its source. In democratic Athens, for example, only men were allowed to vote, not women, and certainly not slaves. Modern democracies, though still not perfect, have strived to abolish this injustice. But in effect, we human beings are not the only living and conscious beings upon Earth. What about other beings, with whom we share embodied life, like plants, landscapes, minerals, and animals?

Julius, of course, felt called to speak up for his companions from the Gaia family. 'I do not imagine that we would be called to sit as animals, plants and mountains together with you in your parliaments,' he said with a spark of humour. (Imagine a representative of the cows in the parliament!) 'It is about collective awareness. With developing ecological movements, and later the corresponding institutions, you have made the first step. But we are still considered beings of lower nature, without consciousness, similarly discounted as the women and slaves of Athens. Consequently, we are not considered evolved enough to speak up for our rights and to propose—from our point of view—proper ways on how to manage the living organism of the Earth.'

Ruth, speaking for those whom we call our ancestors and descendants, expressed dissatisfaction with the model of modern democracy, stating that they too are part of humankind. 'You have left the living organism of planet Earth in a horrendous state, with many unresolved problems. We, as your descendants, will come "down" to the Earth and perhaps find conditions that will ruin us for generations. It is absolutely clear that our word be heard in the future, and even in the present parliaments.'

After hearing from Ruth and Julius, I felt challenged to give a proposal on how much more effectively democracy could be organized, with the inclusion of both ignored sides. It certainly cannot be solved in the parliaments alone. The real challenge will be in creating new patterns of everyday life of human society, which recognize, appreciate, and include the rights and creative gifts of both these partners of humanity.

The word 'parliament' has roots in the French *'parler'*, meaning 'to talk to each other'. We need to find a way to talk and to listen to one another and then to act accordingly! Our present system of discussion between human representatives needs to be complemented by new, still to be discovered, ways of communicating with the elemental world sphere on one side and the sphere of the spiritual world on the other.

This is not impossible. If we use the holistic principles of perception discussed in the previous chapters, then there is the possibility of hearing the ideas and proposals of both partners' side. We would be able to tune to the voice of the spiritual world for their wisdom and suggestions. Elemental beings, the managers of the worlds of nature, would become the voices of the plants, animals, minerals and landscapes. We can imagine the information gained this way could be entered into parliament, to become part of the discussion/decision process to influence human community planning.

Issue of recycling

It is unacceptable that we are moving towards a new constitution of the Earth and a new culture, and yet we would leave behind a disaster of discarded plastics, genetically modified plants, mutilated landscapes etc. Cleaning up the earth, her oceans, and atmosphere has been a concern of all environmentally conscious humans for many decades. But we have only made small dents in this monumental problem. The task obviously transcends our abilities to solve. Can we expect help from the elemental worlds?

Interestingly, Ruth was the first to step forward, though it is difficult to imagine how the world of ancestors and descendants could help with this issue. She pointed to the message of the fifth Seal of the Apocalypse and my interpretation, asserting that the counter-force had found a way to infiltrate great numbers of souls through the passage of birth upon the

Earth, souls that do not belong to Earth's ancestry. Even if these souls do not come with bad intent, they have no intrinsic relationship to the creation of Gaia and to the purpose of human evolution. Without sensing a problem, they work on developing technologies that are aggressively disrespectful to the life of Earth and its beings. They also have alien ideals and try to convert humankind to behaviour that is obviously not our own.

But she points out that it is not her intent to free humankind from responsibility for the chaotic treatment of Earth by attributing it to some outside influence. It is the millions of shallow-thinking, embodied humans that enable their manipulation by the counter-forces. Realization of their behaviour will certainly be a bitter experience for them and not easily balanced out.

At this point, Ruth asserts that the spiritual world could help by closing down false paths leading to incarnation on Earth. But according to the cosmic law that protects the divine gift of free will granted to humankind, they could act only if groups or individuals embodied on Earth would ask.

Julius was keen to approach the issue from a different side. He pointed to the example of recycling. The modern capitalistic economy sees little sense in spending money to reuse discarded materials. But if the parallel world spheres were to cooperate in the solution of this problem, then we could solve all aspects of the embodied world's pollution and destruction. The evolved beings abiding there know technologies of transmutation (in human terms understood as alchemical processes), through which manifested objects that have lost their purpose for existing on the embodied level, could be returned to the storage of the primeval powers of creation. In exchange, fresh creative powers would flow into the relevant economic processes. He assures us that the elemental world, for example, could help by transporting the discarded material, pollutants and energy towards the proper interdimensional portals for the mentioned alchemical process. But they can not help, of course, as long as they do not exist in human awareness. How can somebody help if they do not exist?

Julius pointed out that a good step toward future cooperation between humankind and the elemental world would be the scientific acknowledgement of the immense importance of the so-called 'micro-biom' (evolution of microorganisms) for the fertility of soil, for the health of humans and other embodied beings, and for life in general. 'Similarly as you used horses, not that long ago, for transport, you could cooperate with the microbes. We work with them because they are able to connect directly with the manifested levels of life on Earth, where we cannot. They are not our "horses"; but in a way, they are us, embodied at the manifested level. We are one.'

For our conversation on the issue of recycling, I chose another part of Venice called Sacca Misericordia. It is a small urban haven now used for storing yachts.

Its name in Italian means 'Sack of Mercy'. I previously had geomantically explored the place and the church Madonna Val Verde that stands at its edge. I perceived that the strange name of the place refers to high beings from the angelic network that lament over the destiny of humankind. They want to help humanity, lost in its crumbling creation, but the law of free will prevents them from entering the scene. All they can do is send waves of compassion and hope that they might be called to help before it is too late.

Matrix of bipolarity

I must confess, the following discussion with Ruth and Julius about organizing future Gaia Culture was forgotten until I had finished the conclusion of the book. I had settled in for the night after completing the book, delighted that I had arrived at a happy ending. That night I received a very complex dream (presented in 'Conclusion') that showed the need for a concluding chapter. The dream pointed to the dramatic imbalance between the feminine and masculine aspects of the primeval powers of creation within the present civilization. The message was that we could forget about creating Gaia Culture if we could not heal the very base upon which human cultures stand. The question was not about the balance between feminine and masculine primeval powers at the individual level, but about the imbalance at the collective level.

I first turned to Julius as an expert on different levels of elemental consciousness, asking him to present the role of the primeval powers of creation in the Earthly universe. Surprisingly he refused to answer saying that in this case we are not dealing with sub-elemental levels of Gaia's universe, but with the sub-cultural level of human society. (I use the term 'sub-elemental' for those levels of existence that represent the base for manifested world dimensions. Correspondingly 'sub-cultural' can be understood as the base upon which it is possible to build cultural overlays.)

Julius stated that human evolution, different from other evolutions in Gaia's Earthly universe, is built upon the cosmic Yin-Yang archetype. Unfortunately, modern human cultures understand it mainly at the psychological level, as the relationship between feminine and masculine qualities, or simply as the relationship between men and women.

To illustrate his statement about the importance of the feminine-masculine matrix for human evolution, he directed my attention to the 10th chapter of the Apocalypse, to a detail that has always piqued my curiosity. It speaks of a mighty angel standing with one foot in the sea and the other upon dry land, offering a little book to Saint John:

'Then the voice which I had heard from Heaven was again in my ears, saying: Go and take the little book which lies open in the hand of the angel whose feet are planted on both sea and land.' (Rev. 10:8)

The explanation from Julius was that, in this short sequence of the Apocalypse, the archetype of humankind as a cosmic evolution is coded. We are an 'evolution of the open book'. Primarily being an evolution of cosmic consciousness, we are primarily based upon the polarity principle depicted by the symbol of the angel standing simultaneously in the water and on the dry land—a symbol of feminine-masculine polarity.

'So I went off towards the angel, asking him to give me the little book. "Take it," he said to me, "and eat it up. It will be bitter to your stomach, but sweet as honey in your mouth." Then I took the little book from the angel's hand and swallowed it. It was as sweet as honey to the taste but when I had eaten it up it was bitter to my stomach.' (Rev. 10:9-10)

This sequence shows the initiation of the human beings to becoming a race of consciousness, based upon the wisdom of balanced polarities.

The polarity between water and dry land became, after it was embodied (eaten) by Saint John (representing humankind), the polarity between sweet and bitter—meaning the binary code balancing between feminine and masculine as cosmic Yin and Yang, but also between the region of the head and the region of the belly, or between logic and intuition.

Ruth responded that the archetype of feminine-masculine balanced polarity, offered to humankind as the base of our identity, makes it possible that human beings become a conscious link between the creations of Sophia, on one side (representing the divine feminine at the level of the Galaxy), and Gaia on the other, thus making the synergy of both levels of existence possible. But it is impossible for humankind to take on this role of decisive importance for the emergence of the Gaia Culture, as long as we allow the massive misuse of masculine–feminine polarity at this deep level we are discussing.

Both poles have been torn apart and changed into a dangerous pattern of duality, a constant battle between 'bad and good' sides. After both poles have been separated, individuals and nations grab for wealth, power, and dominance over others through the misuse of the masculine part. The feminine part is celebrated as a source of procreation, while at the same instant, pushed to the brink of the creative processes and misused as a source of sexual delight.

I understand Ruth saying that as long as we allow such a misuse of our identity matrix—that we share with our ancestors and descendants—there is no chance to build the desired Gaia Culture. Also, communication between both halves of humanity is only possible under special conditions. I promised her that I will work on clearing and balancing the feminine/masculine matrix in the framework of my telepathic Cyclic Workshops that take place at the cardinal points of the year.

This was the last meeting with my partners relating to the theme of the emerging Gaia Culture. I wish to conclude it with our gratitude to both of them expressed also in the name of the potential readers of this book.

EXERCISES 4

With Michael messages

As the year changed from 2020 to 2021, the source of the messages received by Andrea Rosslan-Brandt changed. Instead of Gaia messages, Andrea started to receive messages from Michael. This certainly has to do with my decision to ask Michael to be our guide while exploring the parallel worlds of Gaia in the next section, Part 5, of our book.

In Part 5, Michael is presented as a cosmic individual that has, in the recent phase of human development, taken over the task of mediating between humankind and Gaia, the creator of the Earthly cluster of worlds. In this sense we can understand and honour his work as one of the teachers of humankind.

I
III
III
5.1.2021

05.01.2021

Human beings—become more and more
aware of your steps,
of your deeds.
Stay alert during your awakening
and whenever you are connected
with the spiritual realm.
(Michael)

- While sitting, imagine there is a high, thick wall in front of you.
- The wall is so close to you that your knees can feel its coldness.
- For a moment you feel despair, for it seems that your path to the future is blocked.
- Then imagine turning around, standing up, and walking in the opposite direction.
- There is no wall to stop you—only the inspiring beauty of nature.
- Your despair is gone.
- Then imagine turning around to look upon the wall.
- The wall is gone! The path in front of you is open!
- Rejoice!

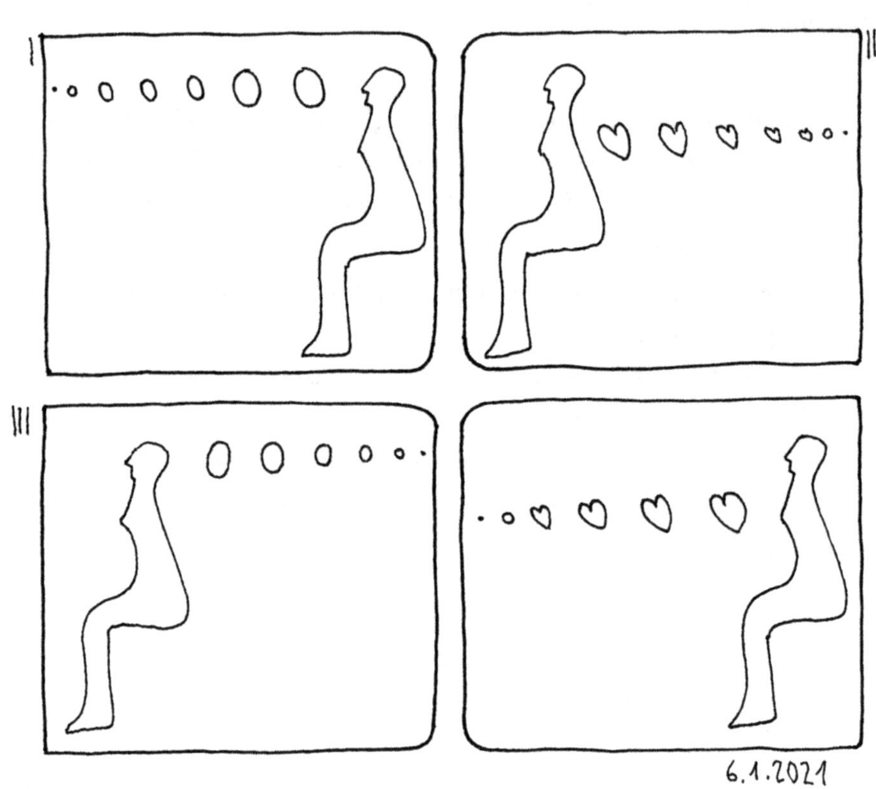

6.1.2021

06.01.2021

Spirit beings in human bodies—
transformation has begun,
—these times.
Resurrect
to live in yourselves
that inner gift that is the heart's thinking.
Allow yourselves to nourish your mind
out of your heart.
Gaia bestows herself on you
and accompanies your metamorphoses.
Follow bravely a new way
and leave the old paths.
Trust in the new that is unknown
and gratefully look at the old
that is fading away.
(Michael)

- Sit down for a moment in peace.
- Then imagine your head walking forward to get in touch with the future human matrix. How does it feel?
- After the head has come back to its place, your heart walks backward to connect with the wisdom gathered through millennia of human development. How does it feel?
- After the heart has come back to its place, your head walks backward to connect with the wisdom gathered through millennia of human development. How does this feel?
- After the head has come back to its place, your heart walks forward to get in touch with the future human matrix. How does it feel?
- After the heart has come back to its place, become aware of the vertical alignment of the brain cavity, the cavity of thorax, and the belly cavity.
- Feel the brain rooted in your heart and your heart rooted in the cavity of the belly. How does this feel?

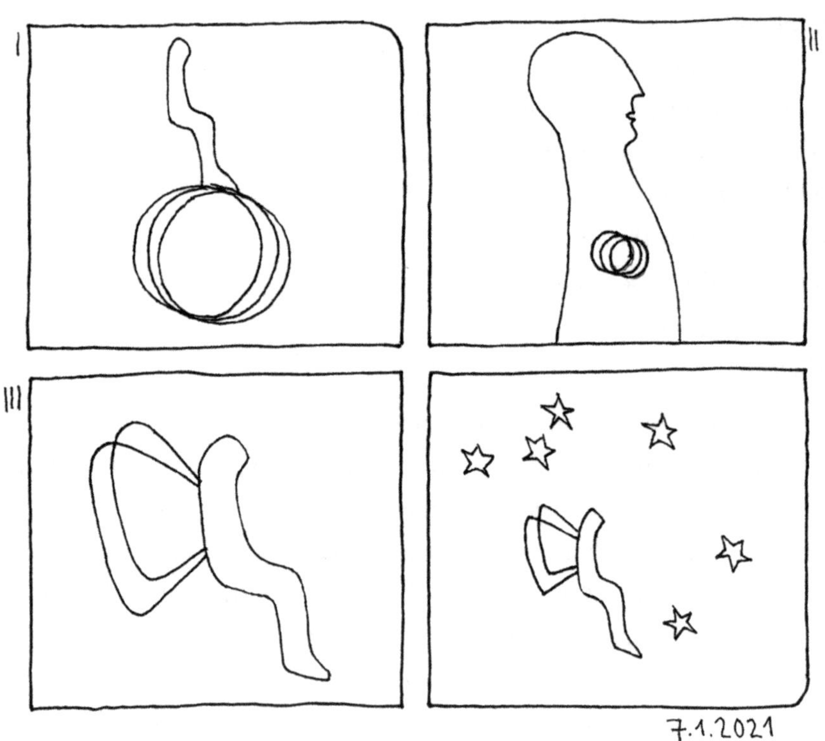
7.1.2021

07.01.2021

Human being, reach out
to Gaia, her beings
and your fellow humans.
The new path is a
path of connectedness.
It is created in the spiritual realm
which you people of our time
dare to enter during this period.
This time is a gift from Gaia.
Reach out your hand, human being,
and accept it gratefully.
Hold it,
cherish it,
Protect it.
(Michael)

- Imagine that you sit with feet positioned upon the Earth globe as it appears when observed from a satellite.
- You feel the globe under your feet adjusting to find its proper position, in tune with the present cosmic moment.
- When the proper position of the Earth globe is found, become aware of a smaller globe searching for the proper position within the space of your heart. It represents your inner compass.
- After your inner compass has found its proper position, imagine that you receive two wings—like a butterfly.
- Move your wings until you are in tune with the cosmic matrix of the given moment, in the process of the universal change.

8.1.2021

08.01.2021

Human beings—
Your wilful decision
to maintain your spiritual connection
with Gaia and her beings
is needed more than ever.
Use your abilities
to enter the spiritual dimensions.
(Michael)

- While sitting, lean a bit forward. Imagine somersaulting three times down into the Earth.
- You arrive in a cave inside the Earth. The walls are covered with beautiful crystals.
- Sitting in the cave, you adjust yourself so that you sit exactly under yourself sitting on the surface.
- Feel how perfectly you are in resonance with Gaia. Enjoy the resonance between the two of you.
- Now imagine that you simultaneously stand upon your shoulders.
- Make this version of yourself as tall as is needed to come into resonance with the spiritual worlds.
- Feel the quality that comes into being if all three aspects of you are in tune with each other.

10.1.2021

10.01.2021

Human beings—
again and again
you are shaken
by the events on the outside.
Take action to discontinue
the tearing apart
which is caused by this—
'through your inner path'.
Wilfully and actively preserve
the spiritual realms of
Gaia and her beings.
(Michael)

- Human beings can be compared to the retort that alchemists use in their purification processes.
- The water in the retort is more or less impure containing effects of past deviations from your personal path.
- Imagine the water of your path positioned in the retort over the fire of inspiration, held upright by Gaia and her elemental helpers.
- While heated, the water of life evaporates and is condensed into a bowl as pure water—containing none of your deviations.
- Take enough time to feel this process of purification within.
- Then take the bowl of pure water, rise high over the Earth, and pour drops of the distilled water over several places on the globe that need healing.

11.1.2021

11.01.2021

Human being,
let me address your spirit.
You are free.
Decide freely for yourself.
It is a potential step
that reveals itself to you
here in contact with Gaia.
Christ in you—
peace awakens,
the new becomes accessible.
(Michael)

- Imagine the human being as a cosmic spinning spindle.
- Imagine the upper point as high as you can reach above your head.
- The lower point is in the Earth just below your feet.
- The axis that connects both points, representing Heaven and the Earth, runs along your backbone.
- Decide in which direction you want to spin.
- Do it in your imagination departing from both extreme points of the axis.
- Your heart-centre, with the decisive role, is centred between the two points.
- At the level of the heart, the spinning expands horizontally, while both points of the vertical axis grow high and deep to gradually reach infinity on both sides.
- The horizontal waves—a result of the spinning movement—touch all beings close and distant with the love of your heart.
- They touch beings of nature and elemental worlds of Gaia; they touch your fellow human beings.
- They inspire them to reconnect with the Earth and Heaven in their own hearts.

14.1.2021

14.01.2021

Human being—
free yourself
from the illusion of your imprisonment.
Use your spirit,
your possibilities to take effect
in the elementary worlds.
Everything is in place.
You and the other humans
are being awaited,
always have been.
Now begins the time
when you are able
to acknowledge this
ever more consciously.
(Michael)

- Imagine sitting in the sand of the lower half of an expired hourglass.
- You feel stuck in old patterns; nothing moves.
- Then the cosmic clock initiates a new age of evolution. Like a strong wind, the change arrives, turning the hourglass upside down.
- You find yourself upside-down in the upper part of the hourglass, head down and feet up.
- Your body is too bulky to follow the change and graciously flow into the free space of the New that is now below.
- To be able to enter the New through the narrow hole of the hourglass, you need to translate yourself into the elements of your matrix.
- One after another your matrix elements descend into the empty space of the new era of human evolution.
- Put yourself together again and see how it feels to be new.

15.1.2021

15.01.2021

Human beings—
it is time.
Your awakening into your spiritual abilities
is vital for the process of the transformation of Gaia,
of her beings,
and also of your surroundings.
Embrace your very own awakening within
and accept your potential.
Each one for himself and
also in your communities.
(Michael)

- Imagine looking through a window. You are surprised to see a huge sleeping volcano.
- A moment later, looking through the same window, you see that a number of small active volcanoes have begun to erupt around the huge sleeping one.
- The sleeping volcano represents Gaia's restraint from introducing unrestrained cataclysmic changes upon the planet.
- Imagine the increasing number of small volcanoes as the new way of introducing changes that becomes possible through cooperation of human individuals and groups collaborating with Gaia, making relatively peaceful changes possible.
- Feel how such a small-scale volcano exists also within your being. Where is it positioned within your body?
- What is the quality that your erupting volcano represents for your contribution to the successful Earth and humankind changes?

PART 5: COOPERATION WITH PARALLEL WORLDS

The Earth's cluster of worlds

In my discussions with the representatives of the elemental and spiritual beings about the importance for the further development of humanity, often the need was mentioned for cooperation with the parallel worlds. What do I mean by the expression 'parallel' or 'synchronic' worlds?

Since the Renaissance, we have come to believe that we live in a spherical bubble we call Earth. The logical mind has convinced us that there is nothing outside of this bubble. My experience in geomantic work in contrast teaches me that the material bubble, while we appreciate its uniqueness, is only one of several world spheres, constituting a cluster of Gaia worlds. Gaia has created a variety of diverse world spheres, each providing an optimal place for development and learning for beings that have decided to accept her hospitality to evolve within the world bubble offered to them—the human race being only one of these.

Together with dolphins, whales, and animals, humankind chose to develop through experiences collected within a world sphere best identified as materialized or embodied. This of course is only partly true; the reality is, we and our other material partners split our time between two world spheres. In the case of humankind, we cycle back and forth between the spiritual and the incarnated bubbles. Something similar goes on with the other mentioned evolutions, yet in a different way of course; later perhaps more about them.

It needs to be clearly stated that the Earth has always existed as a cluster of relatively autonomous worlds. It is only in our relatively recent timeline that rational knowledge became a belief system, a kind of religion of amnesia. Our past connections with the parallel spheres were suppressed and forgotten, and the illusion, asserting that our material sphere is the only living planet in the universe, took power over human awareness.

One world sphere that needs to be highlighted is the one that maintains the base of the entire Earth cluster. Within her own sphere, Gaia has created a 'private' world, composed of minerals, microorganisms, fungi, viruses, plants, elemental beings and landscapes. This is the world bubble that she shares with incarnated animals, humans, whales and dolphins. But also, this 'private' world sphere is in effect a cluster of its own, composed of different world spheres, such as those of dragons or elemental beings.

The closing of humankind into a single world bubble is pure illusion, fabricated by the rational mind, and only functional in a simple one-dimensional reality. We exist simultaneously in at least two of Gaia's cluster of worlds, plus maintain relationships to other member spheres of the Gaia cluster.

The purpose of this portion of our book is to visit some of the world spheres belonging to Gaia's cluster—I often call her the Earthly universe—and to discover how the future and present-day collaboration between us can enrich both humankind and those evolutions settled in the parallel worlds. The process of creating Gaia Culture will enable us all to enter an age of mutual inspiration and joyous cooperation.

Looking for a guide

I have acquired substantial knowledge of the Gaia cluster of parallel worlds in my last four decades of geomantic and Earth healing work. My insights are published in a book I wrote in German called *Synchronic Worlds* (*Synchrone Welten*, AT 2011). But I still need a guide while walking through the Gaia cluster because, though we need to feel the essence of separate parallel worlds, we want to also recognize their relationship to the Gaia Culture project.

Since Michael offered generous help to Andrea and me in creating the meditative exercises in a previous chapter, I hoped that he could also be my guide in the present undertaking. He also provided support in my research for the book on the Fifth Gospel (*Christ Power and Earth Wisdom*, Clairview 2019), through messages received from him by my daughter, Ana Pogačnik. At that time he made it clear that, in the context of the recent cosmic changes, he does not want to be called 'archangel'.

The night after deciding to ask Michael for guidance upon the path through the parallel worlds, I had a dream that I understood as an expression of his acceptance:

In the dream I am sitting in my room writing the book you read when I hear somebody calling from outside the house. I go downstairs to see who is there and meet a young man of stately posture. He tells me that he comes from a certain island that I know—but I cannot remember its name. I try hard without success. Embarrassed I speak out the name of an island in the Adriatic that I know well, but the answer is no. Meanwhile, I notice two younger men and a woman accompany the young man. I excuse myself to return to my writing. I shake hands with the man I consider to be Michael, and with his three companions that I feel to be his students, and run up the stairs to my room.

Only later, after waking, I understood that I could not remember the name of the island because it is not an island at all. An Island without a name is a symbol of another world sphere. And the 'Island' residence of my visitors is most certainly the spiritual world.

I also realized that Michael did not want to be my personal spiritual guide but is ready to guide us through the cluster of Gaia's synchronic worlds. I am aware that my experiences of those worlds would alone not provide a complete image of their constitution and purpose.

I wish to point to Andrea's messages from Michael, from previous and present chapters. They reveal Michael as a cosmic individual that has, in the recent phase of human development, taken over the task of mediating between the spiritual realms, humankind and Gaia—the creator of the Earthly cluster of worlds. In this sense we can understand and honour his work as one of the teachers of humankind. His task is not an easy one, considering the gap that has recently deepened between Gaia and humankind, not to mention the gap between humanity and the spiritual dimensions. I am grateful for his guidance in leading us through the parallel worlds.

The parallel world of stones and minerals

Since I am by profession a sculptor working mainly in stone, I expressed a wish to be led first through the world sphere of stones and minerals. Working with stones, I have discovered that they are beings of consciousness. It is relatively easy to approach that level of their existence. For this purpose I use a simple Gaia Touch perception exercise using the five fingers of both hands:

- Standing in front of a stone, connect the fingers of both hands in front of your plexus area, so that their tips are all united in one point.
- Then open the hands swiftly to left and right, fully, as if you would say to the stone to open itself.
- Repeat the gesture two or three times and then enter into the space of its consciousness.

As our capacity to think belongs to our embodied world dimension, so does stone-consciousness belong to its own manifested level— though it is in a different form from the way humans think and express. In the case of stones, it is a consciousness of perfect silence, free from boundaries. The consciousness of a rock, for example, floats as a large cloud encompassing and permeating the rock. Unable to express outwardly, the stony intelligence instead has great capacity to store information inwardly—a quality that modern human culture implements, and to a great extent misuses in the silica computer chip industry.

Beyond their existence in the manifested dimension as material-ized consciousness, stones, crystals, and minerals also have their own spiritual world sphere. This assertion was completely new to me, a revelation by my guide, Michael. He took me by the hand and led me through the empty spaces, between atoms of the stone's material body, to enter another dimension. I experienced it in awe. The space was filled with different layers of colours and micro-lightning, probably derived from the world of crystals. I did not have the feeling of having entered another dimension related to a specific stone. Rather, we found ourselves in a space common to all stones, minerals, and crystals of the Earth. It had the form of a sphere, giving the impression that each unit of stones, crystals, and minerals is connected to this wondrous inner space.

I next had the feeling of traffic, moving with the speed of light between the archetypes of the mineral kingdom stored in this spherical space and the manifested mineral layers of the Earth. It felt as if the elemental beings of the Element-Earth—traditionally called dwarfs—ran along these lines to feed the consciousness of minerals, stones, and crystals, the matrix of their existence. If this were not being done, then their materialized forms would disperse into a mist of separate atoms. As a result, all the embodied beings of the Earth, the Earth included, would instantly be deprived of their bodily existence.

Facing the wondrous world of minerals, I turned to my guide with the question of what this discovery had to do with future Gaia Culture. He answered with two points:

> Once the communication between the archetypal and manifested aspects of the multidimensional reality is accepted, in other words, not blocked by rational logic, then it will become natural for stones to move in correlation with their changing matrix. This will soften the transition of the materialized Earth body from the linear, 3D, constitution we follow today, towards a body that is integrated in the cluster system, communicating naturally with its synchronic world spheres.

Interdimensional communication will also make much of today's technologies obsolete. It will become possible to move things with simple tools in cooperation with the intuitive, newly developed capacities of our consciousness. Such technology could be used to remodel a landscape or to build a city, but will only be possible with collaboration with the sphere of elemental beings responsible for the modelling and remodelling of manifested reality.

The sphere of viruses

Since I am writing this book in the time of transition between two years (2020/21), when a virus a thousand times smaller then a grain of sand has laid waste to our planetary economy and social life, I am, of course, interested in the place of viruses within the Earth cluster. They are considered to be the oldest manifested beings upon Earth who, even today, after billions of years, are the basis for maintaining and evolving the body of Earth and her embodied life.

If we want to proceed with exploration of the Earth cluster we should be aware, Michael states, that Earth's synchronic worlds are not a cluster of balls, like grapes, that are scarcely connected with each other. We exist in a multidimensional space that offers different possibilities. In some cases separate 'balls' of the parallel worlds are relatively autonomous. They are connected with other bubbles with the help of interdimensional portals. In other cases, like the world of viruses, they intersect and permeate several other spheres of the cluster.

> While viruses permeate the whole of the manifested world, they exist in one form, one sphere. They do not have their own parallel world like humans or animals for example, who move back and forth between the spiritual and manifested spheres. They are present in their entirety, but extend through all living worlds of Gaia. They represent a kind of nirvana of manifested reality. Fighting viruses and declaring them poisonous and destructive is a crime against life. [The name 'virus' comes from '*veneno*', 'poisonous' in Latin.]
>
> If you as humankind presently suffer under a specific kind of virus, then it is a result of your extreme alienation from the archetypes of universal life. Viruses protect the basic tissue of life so that it can never be destroyed. Your way of thinking and the technology that you have developed in the last decades threaten the very existence of life in the Earth cluster, so you must face the corresponding reaction of the virus community.

Viruses, in cooperation with microbes and fungi, represent the fantastic possibility for the tissue of life to appear at the materialized level of reality. Viruses build the basic network upon which the organism of life rests and develops. Microbes are responsible for the next step during which the organism of life manifests. Through their activity they make the expression of life in all its different forms and levels possible. Fungi are next in the process. They translate the living organism of the Earth—up to this point still invisible to our eyes—into visible and manifested forms. Viruses and microbes cannot be seen, but mushrooms are visible and can even be collected and eaten. All three communities of microorganisms together make life on Earth not just possible, but enable it to breathe, develop and to blossom.

The dragon sphere

First I must stress that the dragon sphere is not the home of awful beasts with many heads, as they appear in children's books or in the legend of Saint George, the dragon-killer. Relating to pre-patriarchal myths about dragons as belonging to the archetypes of the Earth, I know dragons as representing the primeval powers of creation at the Earthly and cosmic levels. The life-sustaining role that viruses embody at the manifested level is similar to the task that dragons perform at the more basic causal or archetypal levels.

Since in the Christian iconography Archangel Michael is often pictured together with a dragon, I ask my guide Michael how he would present the dragon sphere as one among the synchronic worlds.

As first Michael showed to me the underground function of the dragon sphere. He led me to a place behind my back, into the depth of the universal creation. I found myself within an extended labyrinth that seems to be without end. The channels of the labyrinth had a certain rhythm of angular and curved forms that do not repeat but are always different. I understood that the sequences of the dragon power move, one after another, through these channels that stand for the matrix of cosmic creation. In this way the primeval powers called 'dragon' keep the cluster of world spheres—not only for the Earth—in existence, alive, and in tune with the cosmic clock.

I was then taken to the top of the universe to see all its star systems and galaxies. It appeared as the shape of an egg. I saw a snake wrapped around this cosmic egg. From this perspective I understood that the cosmic task of the dragon sphere was to hold the basic structure of the universe—the eggshell as its symbol—upright, constantly renewing it so that different star and planetary systems, all with diverse culture and life processes, could thrive. It was obvious that it was not the task of the dragon sphere to interfere with different stars and their clusters of worlds, but rather to offer a basic atomic structure, making the creation of stars and their worlds possible. This is the reason why I saw the snake wrapping the egg from outside, as permanently weaving the basis for creation.

I was then brought down to the manifested Earth. Here the next surprise awaited me. Through Michael's eyes I saw everything in the landscape moving; the trees and forests, the mountains, even the buildings and cities were moving. By observing our world from the parallel reality of the dragon sphere, I was able to observe this otherwise invisible chain of changes taking place.

So called 'dragon lines' come to mind, in the West referred to as 'ley lines'. They represent a manifestation of the primeval powers of creation, continuously moving through the winding corridors of the above-mentioned underground labyrinth. As a result, the dragon lines move landscapes, oceans, and continents in a dance of change, of decomposition and recreation. From the level of the dragon sphere, entirely encompassing the Earth sphere, you would see that nothing ever stands still, or any form remains constant.

The dragon powers were named 'Atom', by the ancient Greeks; in their language defined as the basic component of manifested reality that can 'not be divided'. The terrible images and consequences of an atomic bomb explosion display the immense power stored in a single atom; *this is the dragon power!*

The evolution of elemental beings

Elemental beings are called 'elemental' because, in Western tradition, they work in the classical four elements: Water, Fire, Earth and Air. Chemical science identifies elements from another point of view, as building blocks of the physical world. Yet alchemical tradition understands Water, Fire, Earth and Air as living and conscious units that compose our complex—not just physical or material—manifested reality.

Eastern tradition adds a fifth to these four—metal, formed by the melting of natural ore, using human knowledge of metallurgy. Alternatively, in the language of the West, we speak of the fifth Element as when human culture and the elemental world cooperate. The beings of the fifth Element, for example, are especially active in this time of transition, to awaken humankind to the need of transformation and to help us adjust to the new conditions of embodiment.

When thinking of the elemental world, we usually consider only the half symbolized by mythical beings like sylphs, fairies, dwarfs etc. They represent the manifested half of the elemental sphere. I call it 'manifested' even if the elemental beings do not appear in an embodied form. But they have an important role to play in the process of manifesting the world that we know as our natural environment. We spoke already about this aspect of the elemental beings in the third part of the book. They hold the knowledge of assembling the building blocks of the manifested world to appear in the distinct forms of minerals, plants, animals, human beings, landscapes, biotopes etc.

In order to work with the entire diversity of the living Gaia organism, they had to develop capacities to work within the fluid conditions of water, the fiery transformation processes, the multiple earthly forms, the atmospheric conditions, as well as with human cultures. To enable working within the relatively dense forms of the embodied world, they had to renounce the gift of tangible bodies. Their etheric bodies make possible that they have access to manifested forms and beings from inside as well as outside, thus controlling the inner magnetic power that keeps plants, mountains, animals, humans etc. embodied in material-world conditions.

I have often been asked what happens to an elemental being of a tree if the tree dies. I answer that, in this case, the elemental being would be free to return to the second phase of the elemental hemisphere, where it could regenerate and wait for the call from a young tree in need of an elemental companion. In other words, the elemental world has a similar binary rhythm of existence to that of a human, moving back and forth between the spiritual and embodied aspects of reality.

At this point Michael, my guide to the parallel worlds of the Earthly cluster, stated that though there is a similarity, there is a basic difference between the spiritual world of humankind and that of elemental beings. Human evolution is a guest of Gaia, and in some distant future we will perhaps leave the Earth and continue our evolution somewhere else in the universe. In contrast, the elemental world is a creation of Gaia and Pan and belongs to the planet as one of its creative hands. Its spiritual dimension is positioned within the paradise of Gaia's womb. There the elemental beings are born, and there they return for regeneration and impulses to further their development.

Here we find another parallel to human evolution. As mentioned in the discussion with Ruth and Julius, during their stay in the spiritual world, human souls work on their further development. Something similar is experienced by the elemental beings during their pause in the womb of Gaia. There they go through a transmutation process similar to the change from a larva into a butterfly. This means that each time when they take over a task in the manifested world they are a bit more evolved and capable of performing more complicated tasks while serving as midwives of embodiment.

Then Michael invited me to accompany him into the spiritual hemisphere of the elemental world. The experience was like entering a fairy tale. I was given fairy wings and my body became transparent. I found myself in a liquid atmosphere, where breathing was like taking in a nourishing drink, enriched with limitless happiness. I could dance and sing, being part of the sacred womb of Gaia.

I was then allowed to have a look into the region where elemental beings, enveloped in multilayer membranes, went through the phases of their transmutation. There reigned total peace and a deep kind of concentration, as if along with the incoming bodily changes, the novices were listening to the teaching of Gaia. When completed, they would be ready for their future task in the embodied world of nature or human culture.

Elemental angels

Michael's help in furthering our education of the Elemental sphere gave hope that he would also help us with understanding the world of the angels. I intuit that the Angelic sphere might be the cosmic counterpart of the Elemental sphere. Almost all religious traditions speak of these winged beings. Do they have a place in the cluster of the Earth or are they visitors from some other universe? In the book *Universe of the human body,* I tell of a dream that inspired a hint that such beings exist within the Earthly sphere, having once had an important role in the evolution of the Earth's cluster. Later I began calling them 'elemental angels'. Do these kind of beings exist and what might be their role in the process of creating Gaia Culture?

Michael began with a critical remark about the ignorance of religious concepts that do not recognize the world cluster of Gaia and Pan as autonomous universes.

The consequence is that the angelic world is positioned exclusively within the heavenly spheres, outside and far away from the Earth. Angels are presented as winged beings that approach the Earth 'from above', when they are called for help by some members of the human race.

He explained that when an evolution of beings – the angelic in this case – wants to cooperate more closely with Gaia and her creation, they must put aside their bonds connected to the world of their origin and tune to the specific vibration and quality of the Earthly universe.

This situation occurred in the distant past when the assistance of angelic beings was needed for the development of Earth. Their task was to help Gaia in transforming the material body of the Earth into an environment that could be offered to the evolutions of plants, animals and later humans, each inheriting their own distinct levels of consciousness. To achieve this goal the elemental angels worked within the mineral body of the Earth, helping to anchor within it certain cosmic resonance points connecting the Earth body to the galactic universe.

A monotheistic Christian religion promoted God as supreme ruler of the universe and of the Earth. There was no place in this worldview for 'pagan' beings like Gaia and Pan, let alone for angelic beings that choose to cooperate with them. These 'elemental angels' were cursed as 'luciferic' or 'fallen angels' and were declared to be hostile to God and to the angelic world.

> What you would refer to as the 'Angelic world' is a similar cluster of worlds as Gaia's, but existing at a higher potential level. Speaking in your terms, as your cluster of worlds relates to the level of your solar system, ours relates to the galactic level. You would say that your solar system is logically part of our galaxy. Likewise, the galactic angelic cluster embraces Gaia's composition of worlds. This is why we are co-responsible for what happens on Earth, because Earth's cluster is included within our cluster. This means that we are twice present within your world—once as members of the Earthly cluster (i.e. as elemental angels) and secondly as your teachers, helpers and co-creators.
>
> To compare both clusters, galactic and planetary, you will find within our galactic cluster a sphere similar to the one connected with the primeval powers of creation that you know as dragons. At the galactic level you find a corresponding sphere, named in the time of early Christianity: Seraphim, Cherubim and Thrones. Their task is to hold the universal creation upright and to renew it in each successive moment.

What you know in your world as devas, corresponds—still using your language—to the angelic networks of Archai and Archangels. Their role is to hold certain ethical qualities and matrices of development permanently present and radiating throughout the universe including the spheres of the Earth.

Beings that you call angels can be thought of as corresponding to elemental beings. As elemental beings of the universe angels take care of its manifestation at manifold levels and in different dimensions.

Our primary interest while co-creating Gaia Culture should be directed to the elemental angels. First we need to liberate them from their cursedness:

- Start with the imagination of the mythical bird Phoenix and its resurrection from the ashes.
- Similarly the cursed elemental angels pass the process of transmutation and rise purified as co-creators with Gaia and humankind.
- Feel the subtle touch of their wings upon your body.

I can envision an outstanding role of the elemental angels in the ongoing Earth changing process. They could help at that aspect of the process that demands raising the level of vibrations within stones, mineral layers of the Earth, animal and plant evolutions. They can also offer a similar help to us human beings if we would ask for their assistance.

Creative microorganisms

We already touched upon the theme of microbes when focused on the world sphere of viruses. We understood them as responsible for the second step—after viruses—in enabling the organism of life to manifest. Through their activity, they make possible the expression of life in all its different forms and levels, be it in the body of the Earth or landscape, in animal, in plant, or in the human body. Beyond their miniature-manifested forms, do they also know a more subtle level of existence as we humans do, for example, a relationship to the spiritual world?

The answer is certainly 'no'. Like viruses, microorganisms represent one contained sphere, composed of innumerable units, relatively equally distributed throughout the complete embodied world. It is said that in one litre of ocean water there are as many microbes as people upon the Earth.

But there is a specific peculiarity in the way the sphere of microbes is organized. The sphere of microorganisms knows a spectrum of presence reaching from embodiment (in the densest matter) up to a specific form of spiritual presence—not individually, but as a collective. At the spiritual side of the spectrum, microbes exist as huge swarms of micro-beings that carry a certain spiritual quality or presence through the spaces of the embodied world. In this aspect of their presence I call them 'Gaia Sparks'. In this form they carry the spiritual gifts of Gaia, or of other beings responsible for the spiritual dimension of the Earth cluster, throughout its worlds. I recognized this same phenomena when reading William Bloom's book, *Christ Sparks*. In the book he describes hosts of Sparks accompanying the Christ, as a spiritual being they call the 'Avatar of Synthesis', through the realms of the Earth.

The first time I perceived Gaia Sparks was while watching a biodynamic stir—a process when a biodynamic preparation to fertilize the farming land is being prepared by an hour-long rhythmical stirring of compost diluted in water. In one moment during the stirring I saw this curious swarm of beings entering the stir. They caused the lifting of the light of the preparation to a higher level related to the elemental light and consciousness. Nowadays I call them Sparks. Micheal commented:

> Gaia Sparks are sensitive to spiritual ideas and waves of vibrations, carrying them through the subtle atmosphere of the Earth. If some spiritual being—not necessarily Gaia—creates a pattern of blessing directed to a specific situation on Earth, and if its

intent is pure and selfless, the Sparks will notice it and carry it where the given message and energy is needed, holding the message present there, dancing with it as long as it is needed and helpful.

Sparks, as creative microorganisms, know a special collective sensitivity and awareness that reaches beyond any border. Their communities are knots in a network spread around the Earth. If a group of people, for example, meditates creatively, following a specific purpose, the Sparks will hear it and distribute the message instantly, increasing its effect. Of course they can only help if the creating group is aware of and includes the parallel worlds of Gaia; then their work can attract the attention of the Sparks.

The tragic side of the story is that certain human groups or secret societies have discovered how effective Sparks can be when manipulated. They can be used to trigger strong waves of negative emotions, for example, to push masses of people into a state of existential fear—just look at the world today. Such a massive tsunami of fear washes over swarms of Sparks, such that their collective awareness collapses and they become carriers of destructive emotions and ideas.

Please understand the purpose of my words as a plea to consciously and purposely include the creative microorganisms in your efforts when working for the benefit of the living Earth or humankind. By engaging them in creative work, you protect them from being misused. Be aware that even amidst these chaotic situations, Sparks are able to hear the frequencies of your work because their worldwide collective ear also is listening and waiting to do anything positive for the Earthly cosmos and for humanity.

Through the EM (Effective Microorganisms) Movement people have begun to accept the help of microbes in agriculture, their gardens, the kitchen, health issues, cosmetics etc. It is time to also accept their spiritual aspect—Creative Microorganisms or Sparks—and develop forms of collaboration with them, not just to make Earth a better place to live, but to further the creation of the new Earthly universe.

Here is an exercise that can help to connect with Gaia Sparks:

- Build a ladder of colours from the bottom to the top of your body.
- Start at the bottom of the belly with the colour violet.
- Then blue follows and afterwards green.
- With gold you arrive to the level of the throat.
- From there on, the ladder divides into many completely white branches reaching high over your head. At the end of each branch there is a small white ball.
- Let the balls detach from the branches and unite in a constant spiralling movement that represents a swarm of Sparks.
- If you want to experience Sparks, then bring the swarm down closer to your heart region.
- If you want to collaborate with the swarm, start now by giving them a task for the benefit of the Earthly cosmos or for your fellow human beings.

Partnership with the animals

The role of animals in our present civilization is tragically ambivalent. On one side, we are as we are as human beings due to the fantastic gifts that we have received from animals during the last few million years; we have feet to walk, a heart that beats in our chest, we have eyes to see, ears to hear... we come equipped with all we need to exist and create in the conditions of matter. On the other side, animals are, in most cases, enslaved beings, with almost no possibility to follow their autonomous path of evolution. Is there a possible change envisioned for animals within Gaia Culture?

To answer this question Michael proposes perceiving animals as living between two worlds. Their world is suspended between the sphere of Pan on one side and the sphere of the Zodiac on the other. Animals, from the tiniest insect to the great elephant, are happy and perfectly at home in their essence, connected to both sides, that for them represent Earth and Heaven. (Whales and dolphins are another story, to be explained later.)

We already met Pan while pondering the Apocalypse in the chapter on the Seven Seals. Pan was the lamb with seven horns and seven eyes that was able to break the seals, thus initiating the grand process of Earth changes. We indentified the lamb as Pan, the masculine counterpart of Gaia.

Pan can be imagined as a network of elemental consciousness-and-power that permeates the landscapes and oceans of the Earth, thus connecting animals to the innumerable sources of life-giving impulses from Gaia. Different from human beings, whose purpose for existing allows us to be more autonomous in our connection to Gaia, animals depend upon Pan and Pan's network to be grounded. The less evolved a species, the more important their connection to the Pan focus. Animals of a landscape (land or water) need a constant energetic connection with their 'local' focus of Pan-consciousness to allow them, in each moment, to maintain their purpose for inhabiting the Earth as well as their role in their given natural environment.

Unnatural human boundaries created by the exploitation of the Earth, along with electromagnetic radiation networks, have to a large extent destroyed the natural Pan-organized order of the animal universe. The resulting disorder also causes animal species to lose the connection to another aspect of crucial importance for their wellbeing—the connection to their archetypes, symbolized by the zodiac.

Translation of 'zodiac' from ancient Greek means 'circle of animals'. Different human cultures studied the zodiac to develop human insight into the archetypes that govern paths of incarnation.

In this sense the figures of the zodiac were recognized upon the night sky, imbedded in certain star constellations. While gliding through the chosen constellation, human souls were to acquire specific archetypal qualities needed for their approaching embodiment.

My experience is different. Whilst visiting caves that led deep into the Earth, I met the presence of various archetypal animals from different ancient traditions: a giant fish with human legs, beings similar to the Egyptian Sphinx, snake goddesses (from Greek tradition – Gorgons – beings with the snake body and a human head)... They always showed a curious combination of animal and human bodies.

My insight says that the original zodiacal animals represent the primeval qualities and powers Gaia used in formulating the different aspects of her creation before they took the forms we recognize in the embodied world. These forms include various animal species as well as the varied psychic predispositions of individual human beings. Embodying these archetypes makes life for all of us, animals and humans, more meaningful, and happier – in the case of human species, also supportive of our creativity and of our peace with each other.

To provide the evolving Gaia culture with the needed stability and grounding, the relationship to the animal kingdom must be renewed, most importantly protecting the integrity of the Pan-related network of information that animals need for fulfilling life. For human culture it is of crucial importance to renew our relationship with the animal archetypes that govern and inspire the paths of manifestation.

Dolphins and whales

I have not had a chance to meet whales but I have had several profound experiences with the dolphin family. These connections were made while standing at the shore and even when far inland, where not a whiff of an ocean was possible. This seems like a contradiction, but my insight is that dolphins embody such a highly developed intelligence that their network encompasses the Earth and can make a connection even from a desert.

I also need to clarify that dolphins have a similar relationship with the fish species as human beings have with the apes. My insight says that we both are two interstellar evolutions, given permission from Gaia to enter the sphere of the Earth and continue our evolution in the conditions of materialized ambience. We, as human family, decided to walk the evolutionary path upon land, while dolphins (and whales) decided to evolve in water. Gaia and her elemental beings helped them to develop their bodies, relating to the fish matrix, while humans were offered the possibility of adopting the ape archetype.

Michael informs me that the difference between dolphins and whales is not greater than between human races. On the other side, our close relationship is obvious: dolphins and whales can not survive without breathing air and humans also not without drinking water. But still my question is: What does our relationship mean for a future Gaia Culture?

Michael reminded me that, with the transition towards the new spatial condition of the Earth, the relationship between the single Elements will change. Now the elements of Earth and Fire are dominant, but in the future, their complements, Air and Water, will come forward. Element-Air brings the dominant role of consciousness and freedom of movement. Whales and dolphins are masters of communicating through the Element-Water. Whales are known as poets—singing their endless epos, and dolphins as healers—working through water.

Ideally we should develop in such a direction so as to embody a synthesis between the present-day human being and the dolphin. Of course we will not get a fish tail! It is about developing our subtle bodies so that they can breathe and radiate as a means of communication and communion between people and Gaia with her elemental worlds. (See our discussions about the Water-Element with Ruth and Julius in Part 4.)

To experience this new consciousness, I invite you to try the following meditative exercise—repeat it often while walking in the city, driving, on a train etc. :

- Imagine you are walking along a path that leads down toward a lake filled with crystal-clear water.

- Do not stop when you arrive at the edge of the lake, but continue walking until you are fully immersed in its waters. (If you wish, you may stand up and walk-in-place.)
- You are now surrounded by the crystal-clear water. Look around and feel. This is the quality of the new Earth that Gaia has prepared for a sprouting seed of the new reality to develop into a multidimensional reality that will support the emerging Gaia Culture.
- Be attentive to the mini-chakras that appear all around the edge of your aura. They are sensitive to the cosmic and earthly qualities that we will need to integrate within our bodies in order to adjust to the new constitution of reality.

I have discovered these mini-chakras developing along the edge of our renewed water body (renewed 'astral body') while writing a new book, in German, about Venice as the inheritor of the embryo of the new Earth space. They are manifesting in Venice—note that the water city has the form of a fish, in the form of 13 sacred buildings or places that surround the Venice fish-like body. Four of these spots are the locations where we met with Ruth and Julius to discuss the future constitution of humankind.

Are there forgotten Earth spheres?

My question refers to several spheres that seem to have no connection to the reality we live in presently. Yet during my geomantic and Earth healing work, I've had clear perceptions of the existence of at least two of them. At first, I perceived that they might have taken part in the Earth cluster of worlds in some distant past, and afterwards left to continue their evolution in some other star system. But since the Earth transformation process has begun, I realized that at least two of them make sincere efforts to communicate with us, the human family. I presented my contacts with those two spheres in the book, *Dancing with the Earth Changes*. To give a name to those two spheres, almost forgotten in our memory, I call them 'Sidhe' (pronounced *Shee*) and 'Ents'.

'Sidhe' is a Celtic name for a fairy-like folk. Irish mythology narrates that the Sidhe populated Ireland before the patriarchal, organized Celts arrived. They conquered the Sidhe to take possession of the land and pushed them from the manifested world into mountains and underground. During the last decade, several authors published books about their communications with the Sidhe, among them someone I personally know and respect, David Spangler.

I know the Sidhe from experiencing their manifested artefacts from the age when they were still active upon the embodied Earth. One such artefact is the complex of the so-called 'Bosnian pyramids', which includes an extensive underground labyrinth of tunnels. It was here that I was able to communicate with them through intuitive language. They showed me the distant past, when as collaborators with Gaia and her elemental beings, they prepared the Earth for the incarnation of high cultures upon the material level of reality. Complementary, my daughter Ana established a dialogue with the Bosnian pyramid consciousness concerning the present situation on Earth and our role in the process of basic changes within human beings and our reality. Our insights are published in the book, *Wahrheit aus der Zukunft*—German for 'Truth from the Future'.

The second sphere I would like to relate is the home of the 'Ents'. To be honest, I borrowed the name 'Ents' from Tolkien's *Lord of the Rings*. Tolkien presented Ents as ancient trees, with mobility. They were instrumental in defeating the 'kingdom of darkness'. I know them as beings from a distant star that have incarnated into old trees. They can be found in many ancient trees that display clear personal characteristics. I have discovered such trees both in America and Europe. Similarly to we human beings, incarnated in a further developed animal body, Ents abide inside those special trees, in constant conscious and energetic dialogue with their home star. This 'umbilical cord' connecting them with their star gives them immense creative power, as strong in their abilities as those from *Lord of the Rings*.

Michael's commentary says that those potent parallel worlds have broken their links with humankind after the rule of patriarchal societies over the Earth was established. They were worried that their creative powers could be misused by the new and greedy ruling classes and their magicians.

In the last two decades some of the Sidhe and Ent representatives have shown the will and desire of their world spheres and inhabiting cultures, to help humanity in solving problems that we have projected and loaded upon the Earth within the last few millennia. But we can not expect their cooperation to take on practical forms if we cannot sort out the difficulties in which we are entangled regarding human involvement with the dark sphere of the cosmic counter-force (presented in the 12th and 13th chapters of the Apocalypse).

The dark sphere of the counter-force

As we have discussed in earlier chapters of this book, the goal of the counter-forces appears to be one of obstructing the development of the cosmic plan of Earth and humankind. But, observing from the outside, it seems as if they represent a destructive power that has no place in the universal order. The above-mentioned chapters of the Revelation of Saint John do not support such a superficial assumption. They give testimony to the cosmic origin of the counter-force and the reason why it is involved in the present era of Earth's and humanity's evolution.

It is possible that humankind needed a cosmic corrective force on the awakening of our full inner powers under the condition of free will. Before we were ready to build our high cultures, we were still children, our development overseen by mother Gaia and father Pan and our masters in the spiritual levels. After initiation with the fantastic gift of free will, a kind of mirror was needed. The institution of karma works well to redirect us from past mistakes, but it is not effective as a corrective agent in a given moment. In effect, it should not just mirror our false decisions or activities, but should have the ability to give us a strong kick up the bottom when necessary. The dark sphere acts as that immediate corrective body.

This is not the only reason for accepting the dark sphere as a temporary member of Earth's world cluster. Though I explained to the best of my insights, through translation of the symbolic language of the central 12th chapter of the Apocalypse into logical statements, I still ask Michael to help with a better understanding. If Gaia's plan is to develop the Earth into a peaceful place, where different evolutions of the universe can meet with beings of her creation, working together for the highest good of all, then why is the dark sphere allowed to interfere?

Michael's response:

The Earth and humankind are involved in a cosmic dispute about embodiment. During her age-long evolution, Gaia has, with the help of the elemental beings and the angelic networks, created the unique possibility for spiritual beings to receive eyes to see, ears to hear, and hands to touch the universal creation. What a pity that humans take this unique gift for granted, while the ancient goddesses and gods of the Heaven are jealous, not having access to it. Each touch and each look you perform is considered priceless.

Our present dispute is whether humankind is worthy of enjoying and developing the gift of conscious embodiment, or should it be granted to gods that the Apocalypse has symbolized with the expelling of Lucifer from Heaven to Earth. You are now challenged to prove that you, as humankind, are worthy of the gift of the touchable embodiment. If you are not up to this challenge, then it should be given to the old generation of divine beings that want it for themselves.

To understand the dramatics of the moment, you must consider that the initial gift of embodiment is only the beginning of a long process. The incarnation, supported by the animal kingdom, will continue an evolution, with the help of plants, to the fantastic possibilities of embodiment to a water body. Finally, the divine gift of embodiment, as initiated upon the Earth, will reach the level demonstrated by the Christ through the process of his resurrection. After Resurrection, when he appeared in front of his disciples, he was simultaneously embodied as a material and as a spiritual being.

It is obvious that human awakening is needed without delay, to not lose the opportunity to engage in the process of the further development of the Earth and the universe. Gaia with her elemental and sub-elemental beings have brought the process of manifesting life in material form to a high degree of perfection—just look around at the beauty of the landscape and its biotopes. The next step is possible only through cooperation with us human beings, and later cooperation with all spheres of the Earthly universe.

If we as the human race were to disavow the right of embodiment at this point, it could be granted to the ancient gods who would presumably keep it as their exclusive right. It would not be offered to those cultures and beings that follow the development of the new phase of the Earth and the universe.

Unfortunately the dark sphere has been enormously active during the last two decades, pressing human attention into the narrowness of one crisis after another, so that we cannot perceive the true need of the moment. A financial crisis was followed by terrorist attacks, and prolonged by the pressure of refugees, to be deepened by the global pandemic and lockdowns.

There is some hope offered by the 20th chapter of the Apocalypse stating that the dark sphere could be temporarily detached from humankind's present world. The pressure of its threatening and seducing powers would be removed for a given period of time, in the hope that humans would notice the granted free space and detach themselves from their baseless fears. Quoted in Revelation: 'Then [the angel] hurled him into the pit, and locked and sealed it over his head, so that he could deceive the nations no more until the thousand years were past. But then he must be set free for a little while.' (Rev. 20:3)

The Solar and Lunar spheres

How ridiculous! We speak about different invisible spheres of the Gaia cluster and have yet to mention the only two spheres that are visible to our physical eyes: the powerful sphere of the Sun and the beautiful ever-changing sphere of the Moon. I say 'two' considering that we know the Earth as the third visible sphere only through the eyes and cameras of the astronauts. Do these two spheres belong to the Earth's cluster?

If one listens to the logical mind, the Sun is the centre of the Solar system and governs the Earth as one of its satellites, while the Earth is the master of her own satellite, the Moon. Such a hierarchical structure is unacceptable to the holistic view of the universal order. The Sun may have its own cluster of subtle worlds but it is not in our interest to explore them while talking about Gaia Culture.

On the other hand, it would be ridiculous to state that the Sun has no role to play within Gaia's synchronic worlds. It is obvious that without solar light, power, and its loving care for life upon the Earth, the evolution of Gaia's embodied world would not be possible. There is no question that the Sun plays an important role as a member of the Earth's cluster of worlds. But what is its true role?

To answer this question Michael created within me the image of Gaia radiating at the core of its cluster of synchronic worlds as the primeval sun—more like a star. It is Gaia's creative vision and power emanating from inside of the Earth, brighter than the Sun, representing the core around which the whole cluster of her worlds revolve, including the spheres of the Sun and the Moon.

This does not mean that we return to the old geocentric system, even if it appears so at first glance. The Earth, in the middle of its cosmos, is its creator nourishing its beings, worlds, and evolutions with light and love. Gaia is the inner sun of the Earth that connects all the members of its cluster into a harmonious and interconnected whole, being present at the core of each of them as their own inner star.

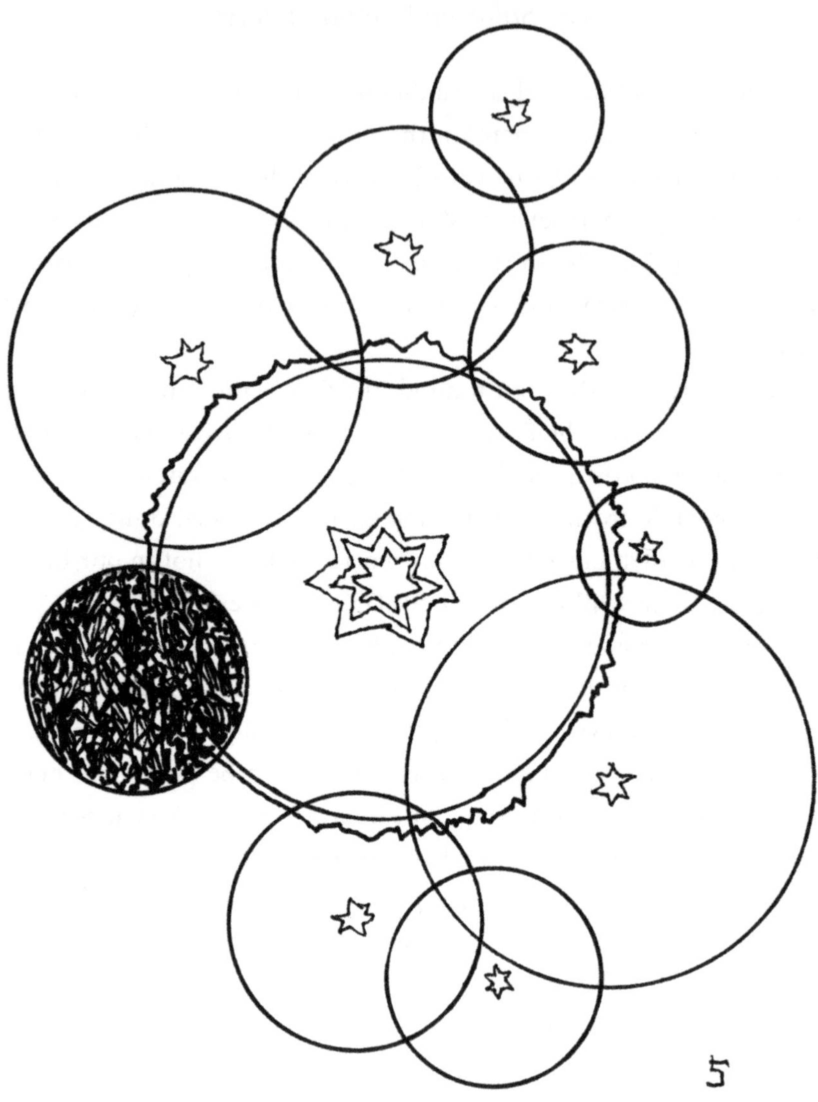

The cluster of Gaia's synchronic worlds—including the dark sphere—with the Earth star in the middle

Losing the central position in relationship to the Earth, how can the role of the solar sphere in Gaia's cluster be explained? I imagine the Sun as the divine Grandmother of the Earth, selflessly offering preconditions Gaia needs to continue with developing her cluster of synchronic worlds. Sun is the power-and-love-volcano supporting Gaia in her efforts to create that mind-blowing composition of partly materialized and partly highly-spiritual worlds. In this sense the Sun can be equated with the 'Great Woman in the Sky' from the central chapter of the Apocalypse.

If we speak in terms of the family constellation, the Moon would be a sister of Gaia. Similarly, as the solar sphere is helping Gaia to hold the planet in permanent movement, the Moon helps 'sister' Gaia to manage the cyclic movement of the watery masses of the oceans. But both these functions refer only to the level of the materialized planet. Tuning to the deeper levels of the relationship between Gaia and the Moon I hear the following story:

> When Gaia decided to take the immense challenge and evolve towards materialization of the Earth, she had to take off all her jewellery—meaning her spiritual treasures—so not to lose them during her billions of years walking through all the cataclysms accompanying the formation of the embodied Earth. They were safely stored in the Moon, because its barren body did not awake the interest of possible robbers. In the form of counter-forces, they search for Gaia's jewellery upon the living Earth.

Translating the story into the present time; it does not mean that 'Gaia's jewellery' stays stored, inaccessible upon the Moon. Through the rhythmical pulsation of the oceans, triggered by the magnetic pull of the Moon, the spiritual qualities of the Earth are being returned to the Earth with each ebb and flow, so to say. With the 'flow', sister Moon takes water to herself to imbue it with the information from Gaia's stored spiritual treasures—water is the perfect carrier of information. With the 'ebb', the Earth inhales the information of its spiritual knowledge, to be stored in the salty water of the oceans. With the help of the etheric water network, 'Gaia's jewellery' is being finally distributed to all beings and spheres of her cluster.

The sphere of Gaia Culture

If we have absorbed all that is presented in this book about the emerging Gaia Culture, then we would infer that Gaia and her elemental helpers are busy creating a separate sphere within the Earth cluster where the new culture can develop in peace.

But when I listen deeply to the voice of Michael within me, I can hear his disagreement with the idea of separate spheres. Instead he draws in my mind a line of a process that shows the relation between the actual Earth and the emerging Gaia Culture that runs through different phases, but always with a close relationship between the two of them.

His timeline starts with the Apocalypse, written in the first century AD, when an important seed of the future Gaia Culture was planted with the help of visions received by Saint John. The next step could be attributed to the formation of the Christian church, built upon the foundations of the so-called New Testament, of which the Apocalypse is its conclusion. But during the proceeding centuries, the Church was fully occupied with spreading Christianity throughout the world, and nothing essential was added to the process. Only with the rise of modern spiritual movements in the mid-ninetieth century—at first through theosophy and later anthroposophy—the inspiration towards building a new holistic culture re-emerged.

Tuning to this inspiration, at the threshold of the third millennium, it became possible to perceive that a new multidimensional Earth sphere began to emerge, which shall be the home of the future Gaia Culture. Its emergence would not be possible without the Earth Changes, talked about in the Introduction to our book, that surfaced at the end of the 1990s.

In the present phase of the Gaia Culture process, the space of the future culture can be perceived as a separate sphere, existing close to the 'old' Earth, and yet completely different, much lighter and happier than the rest of the planet, as experienced by the majority of humankind drowning in the problems of the advanced deterioration of our natural environment and the rise of hitherto unknown maladies.

In the present phase we can indeed speak of two relatively separated worlds, of the 'old' and the 'new' Earth as two autonomous spheres, both integral parts of the same cluster of worlds associated with Gaia. This separation, limited in time, is good for the further development of the new space as home for the future Gaia Culture so that it can evolve protected as if it would grow within Gaia's womb.

But on the other hand, if it leaves the majority of humankind unaware of the background of the cosmic crisis of the planet, then we are left in a rather difficult position. The situation seems hopeless! How can we help those undecided members of humanity to become aware of the frailty of the moment, and the urgent need to leave the old behind—to decide to follow the new path taken by Gaia and her cluster of worlds?

In the present phase of separation, with the Earth spheres split in two, and the human race living within two different world spheres simultaneously, I feel within me the unshakeable trust of Michael that in the future it will be possible to establish Gaia Culture upon the one and same Earth. During the billion years of evolution, Gaia and Pan have developed the materialized Earth to such a degree of strength and beauty—even if now overlaid with human destruction—that it would be a cosmic shame to abandon and replace it with a different sphere of existence.

We should expect that the pull of the Earth's potential perfection would, in the right moment, attract the sphere of the new Earth back to its planet of origin. If the moment of its return were to coincide with the temporary exclusion of the dark sphere of the counter-force, mentioned in the last chapter, then we are not just saved but also blessed.

Anticipating that Gaia Culture will be finally built upon the same embodied Earth we inhabit today, profound work will be needed on transmuting the destructive layers produced by our alienated modern cultures. Like an overlay, they hide the entrance to the matrix of the future culture, which is hidden in a safe place inside the treasury of Gaia.

Michael's response:

> The gigantic work of transmuting the mental, emotional, and cultural layers covering the true Earth can certainly not be accomplished without collaboration and co-creative efforts of the already described parallel spheres of the Gaia cluster and its beings. When the time comes to open (the above-mentioned) treasury of Gaia, you will be surprised that in the last two millennia, while you were playing with your religious disputes, ideological battles, and never-ending wars, Gaia and her co-creating beings were busy creating etheric forms for the archetypes of the future culture, collaborating in silence with different higher evolved humans that have incarnated one after another during these last two millennia.

But this does not mean that the work on creating the new culture is done. As last the archetypes of Gaia Culture have to be one by one translated into social forms, new ways of communication, new forms of art and economy, also everything else that a culture needs to lead a creative and fulfilling life for its members and all other involved beings and evolutions. In this concluding phase of creating Gaia Culture, the divisions between worlds involved in the development of the Earthly universe will be transcended and the project of creating Gaia Culture will become the joint venture of the whole cluster of Gaia worlds.

Thank you, dear Michael, for your guidance!

18.1.2021

EXERCISES 5

With Michael messages

18.01.2021

Human being—
if you allow yourself
a moment of peace,
despite all the hustle and bustle around
and therefore within yourself,
you will unveil the path of new potential.
You will be accompanied,
as soon as you enter
the spiritual realm, with your serenity.
(Michael)

- I am following my usual spiritual path and have arrived at a challenge that seems impossible to master. The feeling is of standing face to face with a steep mountain that is impossible to climb. I am in despair.
- I am then touched by the inspiration to look in another direction and am surprised to realize that there is no obstacle. The path in front of me is free!
- Take the time to feel that you are free and in peace.

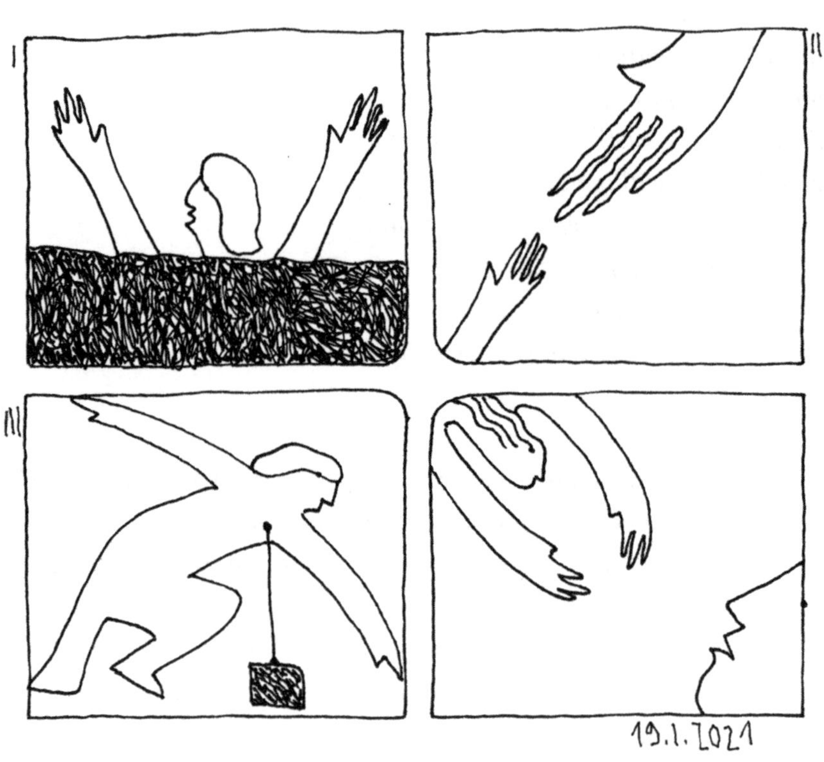

19.1.2021

19.01.2021

Human being—
stay in touch.
Remain present in the spiritual dimension,
do not let yourself be pulled away.
The risk thereof is currently strong.
Find with the help of Gaia,
with the help of your Gaia-connectedness,
your possibilities
to stay tuned in
to the spiritual world.
Do not let yourself be diverted
from our shared path.
(Michael)

- Imagine drowning in a swamp. At the last moment, a hand appears. Without hesitation, you grab the hand and are saved.
- Now try to feel where within your body, in a weak moment, resides the power that brings you down.
- Now try to feel where in your earthly or cosmic environment does the power exist to prevent you from being drawn into dramatic situations.
- Identify those helping being/s and connect with them/it to call for help when needed.

21.1.2021

21.01.2021

Inspirations
are once again touching your heart,
human beings.
Cherish them.
Your Self is waking up from these inspirations,
your stabilizing Gaia-connectedness
allows this to happen.
Proceed further
in this connectedness.
Christ in you.
(Michael)

- Imagine that years ago you sent an aspect of yourself to search for the crystal of truth.
- You have almost forgotten that you have sent this aspect of yourself on this quest.
- One evening you sit in silence in your room when somebody knocks on the door.
- Imagine opening a door inside of you.
- You realize that the aspect of you with the crystal of truth has arrived home.
- Feel the crystal of truth within you radiate with love.
- Share its radiance with your environment and humankind.

25.1.2021

25.01.2021

Human beings—
surrender selflessly
and full of trust
to Mother Earth,
your mother,
mother of all being.
And face
just as selflessly
and trustingly
the responsibility
of your tasks
in the present time.
You will recognize them
in the moments of your devotion.
(Michael)

- Imagine walking a path that leads to a large lake of crystal-clear water.
- When arriving at the edge of the lake you are surprised that the path continues into the depths of the lake.
- You are brave and continue walking the path till you arrive at the bottom of the lake.
- Again you are surprised by how easy it is to breathe in the water, as if the crystalline water of the lake represents an aspect of the new Earth atmosphere.
- Look around and perceive the quality of the fluid-atmosphere and the quality of the world that is imbued with the soft quality of water.

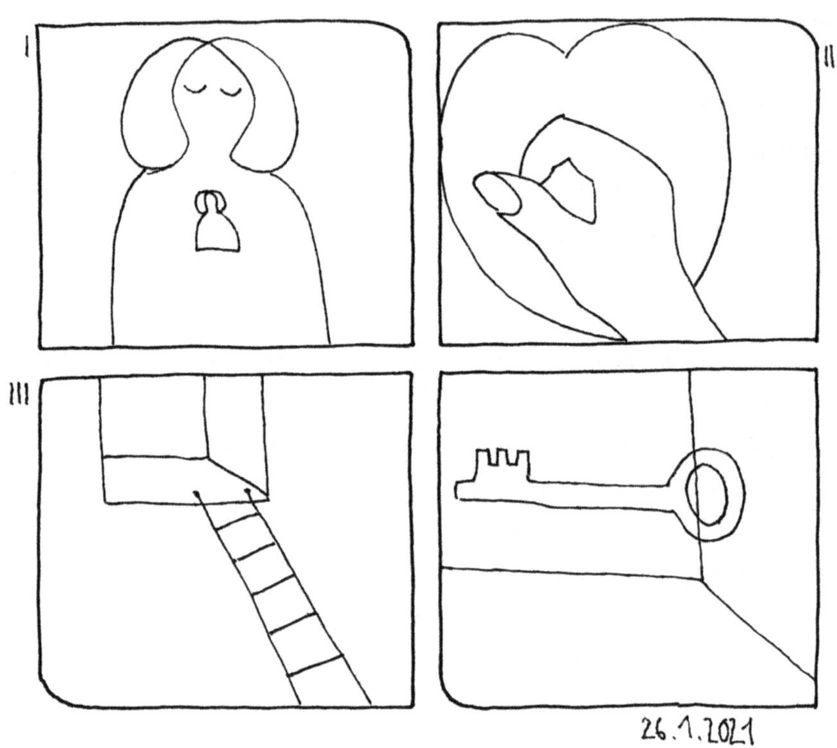

I
II
III
26.1.2021

26.01.2021

Human beings—
it is getting harder
in the current process of change
to enter the spiritual realms.
Become aware:
you need each other as companions.
Have courage
and seek your shared paths.
Be companions for each other.
(Michael)

- Be present at your heart centre.
- Imagine walking from there towards your heart muscle.
- Arriving there, knock at its door.
- After entering, you realize that, besides the four chambers needed to function properly, the heart also has a fifth chamber.
- Walk the stairs up to the fifth chamber. Open the door and sit there some moments in silence.
- Know that if other approaches to the spiritual worlds are closed, here you can always find the key to approach them.
- Try now!

I
II
III
27. 1. 2021

27.01.2021

We need more encounters again
with the quality
of the new shared space
that we created together.
Human beings—take this into account
in all the inner steps
we are currently taking together.
These moves are our preparation
for the required next steps and actions
on the outside.
(Gaia and her beings)

- Imagine a large flock of birds flying high over your head.
- One of the birds unexpectedly turns around and lands in your lap.
- Put your ear close to its beak to hear its message through its subtle voice.
- The instant the bird flies away, a fox jumps into your lap. Listen carefully to what the fox wants to tell you.
- After the fox has left, the closest tree wants to talk to you. Listen to the rustle of its leaves.
- Then the closest mountain calls you to come close. Lean your ear to the ground and listen to its voice.
- At last, your dear ones come to you and want to touch you and be touched.

29.1.2021

29.01.2021

Human being—
your inner peace
becomes ever more essential
in order to go through this time
of transformation with Gaia.
I accompany you—
reach out to me.
Remain courageous and faithfully connected
to your commitment
to be a mediator
while being a human being.
Mediator between heaven and earth—
between the visible
and the invisible dimensions.
(Michael)

- With the lower part of our body we humans are anchored in the peace of Gaia, her forests, mountains, and meadows. But the upper part of our body often gets overcome with fears of all kind.
- Imagine that a white dove comes flying into your lap and leaves an egg.
- Your appreciation for peace makes the egg open and a young white dove appears out of the shell.
- The dove opens its wings and starts to move them while ascending slowly through your body, bringing peace to all its levels.
- Feel its wings vibrating at the level of your solar plexus, at the level of your heart, and at the level of your throat.
- When the dove of peace reaches your head, his wings are so large that they cannot be kept within the head.
- The dove of peace flies into the world to share your peace with your fellow human beings.

31.1.2021

31.01.2021

Human beings—
with your inner peace
you are able to achieve so much
for the peace around you.
(Michael)

- Imagine that you are sitting within the open mouth of a terrible dragon. Its mouth can close at any moment and you would be gone.
- You should not fear. Go down to the chakra under your feet, where you are rooted in Gaia, and bring the vibration of peace into your whole body.
- Listen carefully within. If you feel that there is a region in your body that is not at peace, then bring peace and balance there. As you do so, be especially aware of your elemental heart at the bottom of your breastbone.
- Then look around and realize that others meditating are present within the mouth of the same dragon.
- The whole landscape, with trees, animals, and human dwellings, exist within the mouth of the same dragon.
- This 'terrible' dragon represents the primordial powers of Gaia, embracing and sustaining all existing world spheres.

CONCLUSION: ARRIVING AT THE THRESHOLD OF GAIA CULTURE

Upon arrival

This concluding part of the book was not in my plan. But the very day I finished writing, what I thought to be the last part of the book—about the cluster of Earth's parallel worlds—I had a dream urging me to continue writing. I understood the dream to suggest writing about the conditions that the human community will have to face in the next phase of creating Gaia Culture. The reader would need insight into what comes next on the way towards grounding the new culture, so as to be ready when the next step in the process appears. I believe that it is not a question for the distant future. We are already entangled in the threshold leading to the new era of Earth's and human development.

The dream, to me, concerns our arrival at the threshold of the Gaia Culture. The story it tells is too complex to tell as a whole. I decided to split it into sequences, according to related aspects contained in the dream. In effect, I accepted to be guided towards the conclusion of our book by the following dream:

We travel on a gigantic ocean liner towards Australia. The dream shows the situation upon our arrival.

There are different reasons why my subconscious mind chose 'Australia' to represent the next step in approaching the not-yet-existing Gaia Culture. Australia is the only one of five continents that I never visited in the framework of my geomantic and Earth healing work. Australia is also the continent with the most ancient aboriginal culture, having deep roots in Gaia consciousness.

When I imagine my inner reaction at the moment when the boat bumps at the shore of Australia, I feel a strong wave of change moving through my body, from my feet to my head. I believe the touch of

'Australia', as a Grandmother of the embodied life, is needed when the creation of Gaia Culture moves from an idea to its realization.

More important than our arrival to the shore of 'Australia', is the second message of the dream. It says that in following the different steps of preparation for the new Gaia Culture, we have arrived at the point when a decisive step needs to be taken towards its manifestation. The moment has arrived to step down from the preparatory level to the firm ground of the plan's realization. It may be the most decisive moment of the whole journey!

Some luggage needs to be left behind

The moment of disembarkation has arrived. People take their luggage to leave the boat. I stand up to take my suitcase from the shelf high above the place where I am sitting. To my surprise, my green suitcase is not there. I touch with my hands around the shelf, but all I can feel is a heap of unknown objects lying at the place of my suitcase. I am in distress. How can I survive in Australia without my robe?

I can say that later in the dream I had the intuition to return to that shelf to see if the objects that I touched with my hands were possibly the things from my suitcase, still there, while only the suitcase had disappeared. (The shelf was positioned so high above my seat that I was not able to see what those objects were, I could only briefly touch upon them with my hands.) But I did not retrace my steps to prove that intuition.

The message of this sequence obviously says that before 'landing' we would have to leave behind the patterns that hold reality in a specific form that correspond to the present 3D constitution of our planetary bubble. The suitcase itself was of no use for the purpose of survival. What was important for everyday life was its contents. I was really depressed in that moment thinking, how do I shave myself without my shaver, how do I change my underwear...?—without realizing that all was there; only the old matrix that gave form to the everyday processes needed to be released.

At that point, the dream warned us that stepping over the threshold towards a multidimensional space (a precondition for Gaia Culture to exist in reality), familiar patterns, that help us orient and navigate through the embodied world, may disappear or change drastically. Instead of falling into panic we should concentrate upon the essentials and not grieve the loss of security.

Temporary blackout

I decide to walk around the boat to search for my suitcase; maybe somebody has moved it deliberately. Walking around I realize that all shelves are painted white and made transparent so that I can see that no piece of luggage is left there.

At the time of the dream, I feared the world had been—presumably temporarily—emptied. But the position and colour of the empty shelves told me that, if in such a situation, it would not be a catastrophe, even if triggered by a natural catastrophe. The temporary blackout felt much more as a precondition, to help us realize that we could survive without 'the suitcase'—or even without our material possessions on which we have become so dependent.

As if to help me to understand this sequence of the dream, during my observation of the empty shelves I meet a high–born woman in the uniform of a naval officer who obviously is part of the liner's crew. For a moment I think, I should ask her about my vanished suitcase, but it felt improper to bother her with my personal problems.

My interaction with the woman officer had me believing that the threatening conditions of the blackout should not be treated as a chaotic event, but as a carefully planned action, supervised by the spiritual world of the human race—the spiritual world as described by Ruth in our discussions concerning the organism of the future Gaia Culture. There, the highest evolved souls among our ancestors meet and confer about the best solutions for humankind upon the planet in the given situation and how to inspire humanity to act in the optimal way.

If the liner represents the present situation of humankind, then the woman officer can be identified as a member of the spiritual council supporting the presently embodied human race 'from above'.

Feminine-masculine balance needs to be restored

After giving up my luggage search, I say to myself: if I leave the ship, then I will find myself in an unknown city. It will be difficult to find a toilet. Better I use facilities offered aboard before I leave the ship. I presume to find the toilets somewhere in the belly of the liner. Looking around I realize that two different staircases lead down. But which is the right one? Usually there is an inscription saying 'Ladies' or 'Gentlemen'. I see two electronic boards that should display this information. But they are blank. They show just two illuminated lines and nothing more.

At this moment of indecision, I see a man moving swiftly down the right staircase. Supposing this to be the right staircase for 'Gentlemen', I follow him. But on arriving at the bottom, it seems my presumption was wrong. I see counters, with different food and fruit exposed, as if for sale. Also, ladies stand around that appear to be salespeople. Obviously I have intruded into the 'Ladies' side. So I return upstairs to take the other staircase.

Descending down into the belly of the ship was an obvious symbol that this sequence of the dream related to the primordial powers of creation, the so-called dragon powers. The missing symbols on the staircases pointed out a major problem in the human relationship between feminine (Yin) and masculine (Yang) dragon powers that must be solved before stepping over the threshold separating us from 'Australia'—or separating us from the era when the Gaia Culture can begin to manifest.

After descending the left stairs into the belly of the boat, I am relieved to find myself in front of a half-open door of a toilet. I am surprised how long the restroom's space is, similar to a tunnel. My experience at the end of the toilet's tunnel is too awful to describe. I looked into the egocentric face of masculine self-pride. On the way back I see a group of men having a discussion behind the toilet door.

The feminine-masculine polarization of both underground spaces should not be overlooked. I met women at the right and men at the left side, an obvious problem. The two spaces should complement each other, but instead were two separate destinations with no connection.

But the separation was much deeper than physical. I realized that only the masculine toilet existed, the feminine not at all! The 'Ladies' room', I realized, was reorganized into a brothel! The man whom I followed there did not return up the stairs as I did. And women, I mistook for saleswomen, did not stand behind the counters to sell food, but in front of them as if they were for sale along with the gifts of Gaia displayed on the counters.

As already discussed in the second part of the book, a revolutionary change is required in the feminine-masculine relationship within ourselves, and consequently, also within our cultures. The power that the masculine principle has in the present civilization needs to be shared with the sphere of the feminine. And the feminine qualities of sensitivity and inclusiveness must be shared and accepted by the masculine world. This is a possible way of rebalancing the distorted relationship.

But the imbalance revealed by the dream story had to do with a deeper level of the Yin-Yang relationship that I associate with the level of the primeval powers of creation. The dream brought awareness that the distortion of the Yin-Yang relationship reaches deeper, into the very core of creation. This may be a result of certain genetic engineering or an intervention by the counter-forces. The distortion needs to be healed at the deepest level of existence, a level beyond our sexual polarity.

It is unacceptable for this primordial imbalance to be carried into the Gaia Culture's epoch. It needs to be solved beforehand. This is why it was brought to my attention before disembarking to 'Australia'.

This part of the dream brought awareness of a masculine-feminine polarization, at the level of the primordial powers, that underlies human society and culture. I was unaware of this dichotomy when writing the fourth Part of this book. To be honest, I had to go back and write another chapter that now concludes Part 4. It is called 'Matrix of bipolarity'.

At this point we can not go deeper into my toilet business! It's time to continue our dream.

What about our new clothes?

After returning from the toilet I feel ready to disembark, even if unhappy about having no possessions beside the clothes on my back. But I say to myself, this is the reality, I need to be courageous and accept it. In that moment I notice that I have wrapped around my right shoulder a white piece of cloth. Looking at it more closely I realize it is made of a special material like a shiny raw silk. If the weather is cold, then I can wrap myself into this piece of cloth.

This short sequence of the dream reminded me of a section of my book *Universe of the Human Body*, where I wrote about new subtle layers of our skin that will develop to help us adapt to the high vibrational fields of the multidimensional Earth. Following a revelation from another dream, I wrote about several extensions of our skin layers. Three of them are pertinent to this discussion:

- One is described as a membrane of silvery shimmering threads, composed of a multitude of mandala-shaped units. It would be capable of protecting the body from a radiation overdose or other harmful influences.
- The second layer would be woven from white threads, representing many clusters of body sensors, making possible the simultaneous perception of different layers of multidimensional reality.
- The third layer would be composed of spindle-shaped holes that present a new aspect of the skin's breathing function. I perceive that they would make possible the taking-in of a subtle kind of nourishment instead of air.

If this is not just my imagination, but actually true, then I can indeed disembark without my vanished suitcase.

Insight into the future phase

Encouraged by the discovery of the protective cloth, I go forward to the door to step into the land of Australia. But I am disappointed to realize that I have stepped into an enclosed place. At first I think that it is a corridor leading to the open space of the harbour. But on further examination, I can find no door leading out. The place is furnished like a traditional human home, just larger in its dimensions. I see several people sitting in a curved row as if they are waiting for missing members of a workshop before forming a circle. I instantly realize this to be the wrong direction and I turn around to search for another exit.

Diving back into the dream's image, I realized that the closed space without an exit, in effect, already stood upon the grounds of 'Australia'. In other words, the recent phase of Earth Changes actually marks the arrival of where we have been heading in the past decades. I was disappointed in the dream's message. I was under an illusion that on our arrival in 'Australia', our journey would be complete. Instead, the last sequence of the dream underlined the need for another phase of the process to be worked through before the actual 'landing' could take place. From the dream's image, I understood that we are now entering a new intermediate phase of Earth Changes in which those already awakened members of the human family—including souls from the spiritual world—have specific work to do in the form of some kind of meditation circles using our imaginative capacities.

I received two dreams during the following two nights that more exactly defined the challenges of this intermediate phase. From the first dream I understood that during this new sequence the sphere of the new space will temporarily exit from the world bubble within which we presently exist. The purpose of this stepwise manifested division between the old and the new space is to provide the sphere of Gaia Culture with the needed tranquillity to 'furnish' the space with the future cultural and life forms at the etheric level—a prerequisite for its final manifestation. This is why at first glance I identified the place as a 'traditional human home'.

Till now, both spheres were sharing almost the same reality framework. This was necessary to enable lifting the vibrational level of the 'old' space to a degree that would awaken the dormant awareness of humankind. Yet operating in a combined space was producing too much turmoil, from the transforming and shifting world structures and the activity of the counter-forces to allow the further development of the sphere of the new Earth.

The second additional dream related to my decision to *turn around to search for another exit*. This dream's message pointed out that, while entering this intermediate phase, the primary concern should be to preserve the energetic connection between both temporarily divorced world spheres—the one related to the tangible world and the other with awakened individuals and spiritual beings working for the future Gaia Culture. Otherwise the Gaia Culture sphere could end up totally isolated from the material sphere. This would please the counter-forces; they could finally take hold of the Earth. Maintaining a connective corridor promises the future reuniting of both spheres of reality—as soon as possible—into the new Earth, where the Gaia Culture vision will be able to embody in its entirety.

GAIA CULTURE MANIFESTO

Humanity is intimately connected to Gaia, the Earth's subtle body and consciousness. We are embedded in her streams of life. In a sense we share the same bed with her. Are we aware of this sacred relationship; do we acknowledge our close connection; do we express and cultivate our love for her?

The knowledge of how intimately our multidimensional human body is related to the body of the Earth is nearly lost. Our present civilization is largely ignorant of the consciousness and multiplicity of life of which we are a part. Are we aware that the vital energy systems of the Earth's landscapes permeate the human body as well? Are we aware that the elemental intelligence of Gaia enables us to think, to express emotion, and be creative within the environment of the manifested world?

It is clear that the relationship between the Earth and human culture is so profound that it cannot be 'managed' exclusively by rationally based measures. For example, current scientific and ecological approaches, attempting to address the climate change crisis, do not comprehend the holistic and inter-dependent nature of our planet and its life. In order to develop a culture of co-existence and collaboration with Gaia, we need to transform the one-sided, distorted concepts about who the Earth is and who we are as human beings, and to change our cultural norms and practices accordingly.

1. Who is Gaia?

- Gaia, first and foremost, represents the consciousness of the planet Earth. This consciousness permeates all beings of the Earthly bio-sphere, be it landscapes, animals, elemental beings, atoms, mountains, human beings, microbes, oceans, drops of water…

- According to the ancient Greek tradition, Gaia or Gea is acknowledged and known as a Goddess, to make clear that she represents the divine principle, working permanently inside the embodied and archetypal worlds, to create ideal conditions for all beings, at all levels of existence, and to develop their potentials and express and enjoy the beauty of life.

2. The Community of All Beings

It is not possible to live in harmony, peace, and creativity with the Earth as long as we relate to and manage other beings of Gaia as inferior, as inanimate or without consciousness.

- The manifested forms of life on our planet—plants, animals, and minerals—are not destined to be our slaves, to be manipulated or suppressed as if they have no intrinsic value for the complexity of the living Earth.
- All Gaia's beings, including the invisible ones, represent the senses and portals of Gaia's elemental consciousness through which she communicates with her manifested creation and with the new emerging human culture.
- Instead of institutions and conventions that function only among humans, we are faced with the challenge of creating new supporting attitudes and practices to rediscover and embrace our larger family, composed of all beings present within the Earthly universe. Each member of the emerging Gaia Culture requires a respected and protected place within the new global community.

3. Self-knowledge

We understand that it is not possible to develop a new and mutually fulfilling partnership between human culture and the living Earth if we human beings do not know our true selves in relationship to our core essence.

- The path to self-knowledge is the first step—exploring and experiencing who we are as human beings, as a nexus of different worlds and extensions of life, as an intrinsic part of the evolving multidimensional planetary consciousness and body.
- The next step is learning to cultivate, hold, and maintain one's inner peace, and being centred and grounded in our core essence.
- A third endeavour—without hesitation—is to develop an ethically-based personal practice to guide us in meeting the daily challenges of our planetary world in transition, in relationship to the worlds of Gaia, to our human companions, seen and unseen.

4. The Abundance of Life

The Earth is a planet of extraordinary beauty, fertility, and vital abundance. Today we see a great part of humanity in poverty, diminished and starving. The resources of the Earth are being exploited and managed wastefully and destructively. To address and change this tragic situation, we must transform the principles upon which the planetary economy functions.

- We must restore the cycle of continuous, ongoing exchange between humankind and the worlds of the Earth and nature. The present culture takes from the Earth what it thinks it needs, it consumes these resources, and discards what is left. This is not a cycle of exchange, but a one-way path leading to the spiritual impoverishment of human beings and the plundering and destruction of the Earth.
- To create Gaia Culture we must restore a cycle of exchange between the manifested and causal or archetypal dimensions of the multidimensional Earth—which includes the presently ignored dimensions of Gaia. These dimensions represent inexhaustible sources and reserves of the life force that can renew our exhausted planetary resources, drained by the current materialistic and linear one-way economy.

- To undertake this task we must overcome and transform rational and dismissive prejudices regarding the so-called 'causal or archetypal' dimensions of reality. Let us support efforts to establish a new paradigm that honours the multidimensionality of nature, the Earth and human beings.

5. Education

An essential part of Gaia Culture is to creatively engage in transforming existing systems of education.

- We must understand, protect and nurture the natural sensibility of the child in relationship to all different beings and levels of existence. Human beings whose sensitivity towards different facets of life has been encouraged and supported, can naturally become loving partners of the Earth and co-creative inhabitants of Gaia's worlds.

- Next, the education system should help young people recognize that they are multidimensional beings, playing and creating within an environment that is equally rich on many different dimensions of existence.

- Children can be empowered to distinguish what is true and what is not true, to discriminate and navigate a world where powers of illusion and manipulation separate human beings from their true essence. These powers of illusion and manipulation can become increasingly dangerous with the advancement of electronic media and communications.

- A primary goal of the education system is to help human beings discover and know their purpose and their creative place within the enlarged planetary family, to be in and with nature, so that in the course of their lives, they can contribute to the beauty and richness of life.

6. The Art and Practice of Geomancy

Geomancy represents an evolving knowledge and practice about the streams, energy centres, and circulations of vital forces and elemental consciousness that occur in landscapes throughout the planet. To sustain life upon Earth, Gaia needs these vital forces to be free to breathe and function according to their planetary design. Our present civilization's ignorance regarding these essential aspects of the Earth, all too often block and weaken the proper functioning and vitality of Earth's vital organs.

- The task of today's geomancy is to develop approaches that can help human culture gain insights into and knowledge and understanding of the crucial importance of the vital-energy organism of the Earth, its elemental consciousness, and its sacred dimensions.
- We can participate in the unfolding Gaia Culture by developing and practicing our sensibility and perception of the essence of nature and its elemental and spiritual beings.
- The acknowledged and respected results of such deeper perceptions of nature, places, and landscapes can be incorporated into urban and landscape planning and other related disciplines in universities, into centres and programmes of learning worldwide, and into the innumerable activities that characterize our modern culture.
- We must develop the political, social, and economic means to protect and support those places upon the Earth that are of decisive and critical importance to the health and vitality of the planet and its inhabitants.
- As traditional societies have done over millennia, we can and should create ritual and artistic forms through which the sacredness of these places and the Earth can be recognized and celebrated.

7. *The New Space of Reality*

Gaia, the Earth consciousness, is a dynamic being, permanently evolving and creating new conditions for life, renewing space and time structures, so that all her beings that exist at different levels of life can develop and evolve accordingly.

- Under the pressure and threat that contemporary civilization and life systems upon the planet could collapse, Gaia recently began to create new space and time foundations for the planet to adapt to our present circumstances and to sustain our future development.
- This new space and time framework transcends the boundaries of traditional perception and can be understood as a multidimensional structure and process that provides space and opportunity to all beings, visible and invisible, to live in peaceful and creative interaction.
- The new space is, first of all, an ethical imperative. It is based upon loving, conscious, and co-creative relationships between all beings involved in the web of life upon the Earth and within its subtle places and dimensions.
- The new space of reality is already supporting life on Earth, but we ordinarily do not perceive and recognize it until and unless we dedicate and cultivate conscious attention to its presence.

The Earth, Gaia, with all her beings, visible and invisible, has offered humankind the wonderful opportunity to live and breathe within the world of physical matter, to enjoy and celebrate its beauty and creative potentials. To an extent we have transformed her hospitality into valuable experiences and creative deeds. However, at the same time we humans have also unconsciously exploited the Earth without regard to consequences and without regard to other beings of life.

The time to decide which of these two paths we will take into the future has arrived. The only path that makes sense is to reconnect with the essence of life and embrace a loving partnership with Gaia, the

Earth. This path involves a challenging transformation of our current cultures and may provoke changes in many aspects of the embodied world as we know it, as we continue to evolve into the future.

Marko Pogačnik, UNESCO Artist for Peace
2008-2020

A message from Clairview

We are an independent publishing company with a focus on cutting-edge, non-fiction books. Our innovative list covers current affairs and politics, health, the arts, history, science and spirituality. But regardless of subject, our books have a common link: they all question conventional thinking, dogmas and received wisdom.

Despite being a small company, our list features some big names, such as Booker Prize winner Ben Okri, literary giant Gore Vidal, world leader Mikhail Gorbachev, modern artist Joseph Beuys and natural childbirth pioneer Michel Odent.

So, check out our full catalogue online at
www.clairviewbooks.com
and join our emailing list for news on new titles.

office@clairviewbooks.com